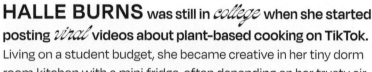

HALLE BURNS was still in *college* when she started posting *viral* videos about plant-based cooking on TikTok. Living on a student budget, she became creative in her tiny dorm room kitchen with a mini fridge, often depending on her trusty air fryer and small blender to make simple meals. Adoring her soothing narration, millions of fans have resonated with her easy yet inventive vegan recipes.

Halle often thinks, *How can I make a crave-worthy dish in the simplest way possible?* That's why *Call Me Vegan* proves vegan cooking can be convenient and failproof with time-saving methods and affordable ingredients found in any grocery store. You'll find a wide range of effortless and experimental recipes such as Hal's Everything Seasoning or Spicy Citrus Vinaigrette, which can be prepared in advance and used to jazz up the flavor of any vegetable. If you're ever in a situation where you run out of bread, don't freak out! Emergency Bread can be baked in a flash in a microwave oven. The book includes snacks that smack like Angry Edamame and Two-Ingredient Pretzel Cloud Bites, breakfast recipes like a Cinnamon Sugar Tortilla Bowl and Chunky Cocoa-Banana Stovetop Granola, and main dishes like her Watermelon Tuna Bowl, Mushroom Pulled Pork, and Artichoke Dip 'Shroom Burgers. It also covers basics like Mixed Berry Chia Jam, Instant Plant Milk, and Tofu Cream Cheese, along with tips for stocking your pantry and essential kitchen tools to get you started.

This one-of-a-kind cookbook will inspire both a new generation of the plant-curious and longtime vegans craving more adventurous recipes that only Halle's mind could create.

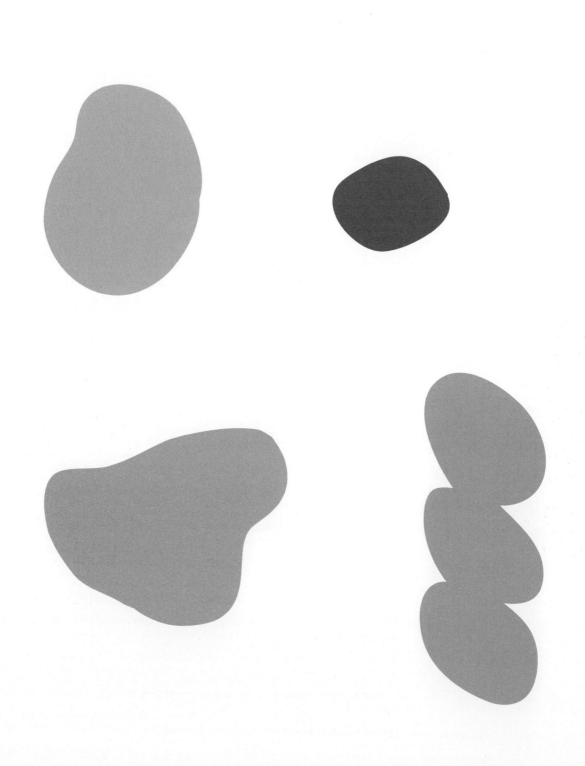

CALL ME *Vegan*

CALL ME

SIMON ELEMENT

NEW YORK   AMSTERDAM/ANTWERP   LONDON   TORONTO   SYDNEY   NEW DELHI

Easy
Plant-Based
Recipes for
Every Craving

Vegan

HALLE BURNS

with Rebecca Miller Ffrench

Photography by Lauren Volo

SIMON
ELEMENT

An Imprint of Simon & Schuster, LLC
1230 Avenue of the Americas
New York, NY 10020

First Simon Element hardcover edition March 2025

SIMON ELEMENT is a trademark of Simon & Schuster, LLC

For information about special discounts for bulk purchases,
please contact Simon & Schuster Special Sales at 1-866-506-1949
or business@simonandschuster.com.

The Simon & Schuster Speakers Bureau can bring authors to your
live event. For more information or to book an event, contact the
Simon & Schuster Speakers Bureau at 1-866-248-3049 or visit our
website at www.simonspeakers.com.

Interior design by Laura Palese

Manufactured in China

10 9 8 7 6 5 4 3 2 1

Library of Congress Cataloging-in-Publication Data has been applied for.

ISBN 978-1-6680-1249-9
ISBN 978-1-6680-1250-5 (ebook)

FOR FRANK

Snacks That Smack

Before Noon

Easy Meals 102

The Sweets Section 152

Vegan Basics 184

HELLO! My name is **Halle** and welcome to *Call Me Vegan*, a plant-focused visual diary of how I cook every day, and *conveniently,* everything is vegan.

And what should I call you? *Plant-curious?* A newish vegan? Are you an **EXPERIMENTALIST** or a perfectionist? No matter who you are in the kitchen, these pages demonstrate how easy it is to create incredible tastes and **textures** (think crispy, crunchy, chewy, creamy, gooey) using minimal ingredients and basic kitchen utensils—not to mention seventy plus of my recipes are gluten-free. *Call Me Vegan* is for everyone.

In college, when I started cooking for myself, I had nothing but a microwave, a mini fridge, and a small blender. Since then, every recipe I've made has centered around the idea that if I can't make it look and taste good in a dorm room, it's not simple enough.

Flip through the pages of this book for inspiration and let me be your guide. If you haven't eaten this way before, try little switches, like swapping dairy milk for my Instant Plant Milk (page 199) or making my Killer Chili with Lentil Ground Beef (page 108) instead of a beef version. And I want you to make these recipes your own. Do you like things a little sweeter? Add another tablespoon of sugar and reach out to me if you think my Mixed Berry Chia Jam (page 223) is better that way. Are my Puffed Beans (page 20) crispy enough for you? If not, bake them a little longer. Who is stopping you?

This is a **NONJUDGMENTAL** space.

This book is for *you*.

I like to look at eating vegan as problem-solving, asking myself, "How can I make a crave-worthy dish in the simplest way possible?" The ingredients for every recipe in here can be found in your local grocery stores, with one or two exceptions that are worth the extra hunt.

My Vegan Basics chapter includes recipes for tons of plant-based essentials like milk, cheeses, spreads, yogurt, and more. For example, if I don't have vegan cheese in the fridge, I make my own with simple pantry ingredients you can find on my grocery list (see page 14). This section is gold—seriously.

Making your own vegan staples is very cost-effective, as vegan processed foods can get pricey. From a simple two-ingredient Tofu Dough (page 216) to my Spicy Citrus Vinaigrette (page 190), these basics are building blocks for other recipes in my book. If you don't have time to make the basics, I offer store-bought alternatives. And now that I've mentioned time, I have to say that my recipes are all pretty fast. Most can be made in 15 to 30 minutes. If you are new to vegan cooking, you could even start with the chapter on Vegan Basics (page 184), trying out some of my favorite staples like Cheap & Sweet Syrup (page 194), Potato Cheese (page 204), or Emergency Bread (page 221).

Don't freak out if this is new to you. These pages are a calm culinary headspace as much as they are instructional.

Here's what you can expect from my recipes:

**Accessible · Craveable · Failproof · Followable
Repeatable · Shareable · Simple**

Just do what I did when I started cooking: find a dish that catches your eye and begin. These recipes will show you how convenient cooking for yourself can be. I promise.

— hal

Halle's Grocery List

Produce and Such

Avocado

Bananas

Lemons

Big bag of spinach
(6 to 10 ounces)

Big bag of kale
(1-pound bag)

Fresh parsley

Fresh cilantro

Fresh basil

Sweet potatoes

Carrots

Cucumbers

Cauliflower

Spaghetti squash

Refrigerated and Frozen

Soy-based vegan
yogurt, like Silk

Vegan cheese slices,
like Chao

Vegan butter, like
Miyoko's

Vegan cream cheese,
like Kite Hill

Tofu, firm and extra-
firm

Frozen mixed berries

Dry Goods

Flour tortillas

Sandwich bread

Rice cakes

Dried lentils

Quinoa

Sushi rice

Old-fashioned oats

Chia seeds

Flaxseeds

A variety of nuts

Nutritional yeast

Panko bread crumbs

Organic cane sugar

All-purpose flour

Cocoa powder

Ground paprika

Ground white pepper

Black peppercorns

Finely ground sea salt

Chili powder

Garlic powder

Onion powder

Dried oregano

Dried parsley

Ground cinnamon

Canned and Jarred

Pure vanilla extract

Canned black beans

Canned chickpeas

Marinara sauce

Pickles

Olives

Peanut butter

Sriracha

Extra-virgin olive oil

Refined coconut oil

My Key Ingredients and Tools

Extra-Virgin Olive Oil (EVOO)

When it comes to olive oil, I opt for one that has been certified extra virgin, which means it has been cold-pressed for a higher quality oil than regular noncertified oil. Extra-virgin olive oil tends to have a fruitier flavor than regular, so choose whichever taste you prefer. Extra-virgin and pure or regular olive oils can be used interchangeably in my recipes.

Refined Coconut Oil

I use coconut oil almost as often as I do olive oil. Unrefined coconut oil has a strong coconut flavor and a lower smoking point than refined coconut oil, which has a more neutral flavor and works well at high temperatures. To avoid any unwanted coconut flavor, use refined, which is what I use the most, but you can use either in all my recipes.

Canned Beans

Canned beans are a favorite of mine because they can be used right away or stored for months. There is no shame in choosing to use them instead of dried beans. They are convenient and get the job done, not to mention they are one of my favorite protein sources.

Dried Herbs

Dried herbs and spices are a hero in this book. I like their convenience over fresh. With the right amounts and combinations, the dried variety can enhance the flavor components of a snack or meal more than you'd imagine from a shelf-stable product. I love making my own mixes, like my Hal's Everything Seasoning (page 187), which combines my favorite dried herbs and spices to be used regularly.

Fine Sea Salt

Fine sea salt—it's what my dad uses in his kitchen, and I'm convinced I can taste the difference between it and table salt. The main difference in salts are crystal size and shape. Some of my recipes, like Two-Ingredient Pretzel Cloud Bites (page 48), call for a little bit of flaky salt for a finishing touch, but most of my recipes call for fine sea salt, which adds a mineral flavor I love.

USDA Organic Cane Sugar

USDA organic cane sugar is what I try to buy, as nonorganic sugars can be processed in a way that makes me uneasy (using animal products). However, cane sugar granules are often a little bigger than those in white granulated sugar. If you want a finer sugar, you can pulse cane sugar in a blender—and if you keep processing, cane sugar in a blender will turn to powdered sugar.

The same processing method using animal products can also be used for brown sugar (which is a mix of molasses and white sugars), so organic is a safer bet there, too. Most often I use maple syrup or my homemade Cheap & Sweet Syrup (page 194) for sweetening recipes.

Kitchen Shears

I use very few kitchen gadgets, but there is one that I use more than others: kitchen shears. I like to cut my Snipped Tofu Pasta (page 127) with them. It's also super easy to chop fresh herbs with shears; I use scissors for my Chopped Salad (page 135). And I find that they're great to trim rice paper for my crispy Rice Paper Bacon Snack Strips (page 28). You'll want to keep these sanitary and for kitchen use only. I have a separate pair of scissors for quarter-life-crisis bang trims.

My Beloved Blender

One of the appliances I call on most is my blender. In fact, a portable blender got me through college. I used a Ninja Bullet for smoothies, of course, but I also used it to make small batches of oat flour, vegan mayo, dips, my Chocolate Protein Spread (page 209), and vegan cheese. If you have enough room in your kitchen, I feel a high-speed blender is worth the investment and the counter space. To make many of my recipes, you'll need some kind of tool with a blade. In some cases, a food processor will work, but a blender is ideal.

My Best Friend: The Air Fryer

It's like a small hot box that uses air and a high temperature to crisp up essentially anything. I can't not include air fryer options in a book centered around convenience because the countertop oven cuts cooking time in half—and often produces a crispier, crunchier texture than a conventional oven. It's kind of like a culinary cheat code. In fact, some recipes are actually better using an air fryer, like my Air-Fryer Smoky Tofu Tips (page 124), which I wrote especially for it. There are plenty of other recipes in this book that work well in the air fryer, too (page 235).

1. SNA

That

S

CKS

MACK

Puffed BEANS

Have you ever puffed your beans? This is probably one of my favorite finger foods in existence. You can use any bean here, but the bigger the bean, the better the bite. I recommend using butter beans, also called lima or gigante beans, so they are big enough to dip. Don't get me wrong, they are delicious alone, as most snacks should be—but dunking these guys in a little creamy dip, guac, or vegan cream cheese makes them killer.

Makes
1½ CUPS

Cooking spray

1 (15-ounce) can butter beans, drained and rinsed

2 tablespoon extra-virgin olive oil or melted vegan butter

4 tablespoons Hal's Everything Seasoning (page 187) or your favorite premixed spice blend

Fine sea salt and freshly ground black pepper

1 teaspoon finely grated lemon zest (optional)

 Preheat the oven to 400°F. Coat a sheet pan with cooking spray. Set aside.

 Using a paper towel, pat the beans until they are very dry, place them in a medium bowl, and toss with the olive oil until evenly coated. Sprinkle with Hal's seasoning and toss to coat.

 Spread the beans in a single layer on the prepared sheet pan. Bake until most of the beans have "puffed" or split, about 25 minutes.

 Transfer the baked beans to a bowl and sprinkle with salt and pepper, to taste. Sprinkle with the lemon zest, if using, and toss. Cool for 10 minutes before serving. The beans will crisp up some as they cool and the insides will stay relatively creamy. Keep the beans in an airtight container for up to 3 days.

Tofu

If popcorn had a cool vegan aunt, her name would be Tofu Pop—a little crunchy, quirky, and kinda spicy. This small pop-in-your-mouth snack is made by rolling a basic, practically universal tofu dough into small balls, sprinkling them with spices and baking until the outsides are crispy and the insides are chewy, kind of like a homemade breadstick. They can also be made using Sweet Potato Dough (page 216).

Makes
50 POPS

1 batch Tofu Dough (page 216)

1 tablespoon extra-virgin olive oil or melted vegan butter

1 teaspoon garlic powder

1 teaspoon onion powder

1 teaspoon dried oregano

1 teaspoon dried parsley

1 teaspoon fine sea salt

⅛ teaspoon freshly ground black pepper

Pinch of red pepper flakes

1 Preheat the oven to 400°F.

2 Divide the dough into small, teaspoon-size pieces and roll into smooth balls the size of a medium olive. In a wide, shallow bowl, toss the balls with the olive oil until evenly coated. Sprinkle with the garlic and onion powders, oregano, parsley, salt, black pepper, and pepper flakes.

3 Place the coated balls 1 inch apart on a sheet pan and bake for 7 minutes. Then turn each one over (as best as you can with a ball) so that the balls brown evenly. Continue to bake until the puffs turn golden and feel firm when squeezed, another 7 minutes or so (14 to 18 minutes total). Serve immediately.

POPS

Popcorn Olives

This recipe is for my olive lovers or want-to-be-olive-lovers who need an unforget-table first olive-tasting experience. Will this crispy, spicy version of an olive convert you if you aren't a fan? I hope so! A heads-up, though: Like many small appetizers, this recipe takes a bit of time to make, although in my opinion, it's most definitely worth it. Don't skip out on dipping the olives in the batter twice because I've tried. Believe me, you want the extra crunch from the double dip!

1 CUP OLIVES

Cooking spray

2 ounces (¼ cup) vegan cream cheese, softened to room temperature

2 tablespoons sriracha

1 teaspoon maple syrup

1 cup large, pitted green or black canned olives, strained and patted dry

⅔ cup all-purpose flour

⅓ cup unsweetened almond or oat milk

½ teaspoon fine sea salt, plus more for seasoning

⅔ cup Hal's Everything Seasoning (page 187) or panko bread crumbs

 1 Preheat the oven to 375°F. Coat a sheet pan with cooking spray. Set aside.

 2 In a small bowl, use a fork or spatula to mix together the cream cheese, sriracha, and maple syrup and stir until smooth. For a homemade piping bag, spoon the mixture into a plastic baggie and snip off a corner. Using a spoon or a piping bag, fill the olives with the cream cheese mixture—this part is satisfying, but a little tedious.

3 In a second small bowl, combine ⅓ cup of the flour, the almond milk, and salt. Pour the remaining ⅓ cup flour on a plate and pour the Hal's seasoning on a second plate. Using a toothpick, pierce an olive and dip it first in the flour-milk mixture and let it drip above the bowl for a few seconds to remove any excess batter. Next, roll the olive in the flour, then in the batter a second time, then in the seasoning. Set the coated olive on the prepared sheet pan. Repeat the process of dipping each olive in the flour-milk batter, then flour, then batter again, then seasoning.

4 Bake until the coating begins to turn golden, 20 to 25 minutes. They are best eaten right away. If you do have leftovers, store them in an airtight container and reheat at 350°F for about 8 minutes before serving.

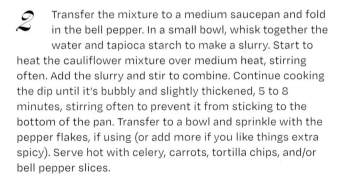

CAULIFLOWER BUFFALO Dip

Makes
1 CUP

8 ounces (about 2 cups)
frozen cauliflower or
cauliflower rice

⅓ cup Buffalo sauce
(I love Frank's)

¼ cup Homemade Vegan Mayo
(page 196) or store-bought
vegan mayo

2 tablespoons white vinegar

1 small garlic clove

1 teaspoon dried parsley

½ teaspoon fine sea salt

½ teaspoon freshly ground
black pepper

1 bell pepper, stemmed,
seeded, and diced

2 tablespoons water

1 tablespoon tapioca starch

Red pepper flakes, for sprinkling
(optional)

3 to 4 celery sticks, carrot
sticks, tortilla chips,
and/or a thinly sliced bell
pepper for dipping

I have been living in the South for a while and have come to know Buffalo dip as an appetizer most southerners can't live without. While this spicy snack is usually made with chicken, I sub in cauliflower for a vegan take. You *could* use a whole cauliflower here, steamed or boiled until soft, but I always use frozen and riced cauliflower because it's so much easier and works perfectly.

1   In a blender or food processor, pulse together the cauliflower, Buffalo sauce, mayo, vinegar, garlic, parsley, salt, and pepper until fully smooth and glossy.

2   Transfer the mixture to a medium saucepan and fold in the bell pepper. In a small bowl, whisk together the water and tapioca starch to make a slurry. Start to heat the cauliflower mixture over medium heat, stirring often. Add the slurry and stir to combine. Continue cooking the dip until it's bubbly and slightly thickened, 5 to 8 minutes, stirring often to prevent it from sticking to the bottom of the pan. Transfer to a bowl and sprinkle with the pepper flakes, if using (or add more if you like things extra spicy). Serve hot with celery, carrots, tortilla chips, and/or bell pepper slices.

3   Store refrigerated in an airtight container for up to 3 days. It can be eaten cold, or to reheat, microwave or warm it up on the stovetop until heated through.

Sexy Tuna SALAD (FISH-FREE)

I eat this almost every day. Mashing the chickpeas with a fork creates a texture that channels real tuna salad. I am normally a big sweets person, but I'm *so* into the pickles and hot sauce combo here. The salad's flavor gets even better as the ingredients meld, so you can easily make this and enjoy it the next day. It's great as a dip for chips, or try it warmed on bread with melted vegan cheese (think vegan tuna melt!).

Serves 2 TO 4

1 (15-ounce) can chickpeas

1 handful greens such as bagged spinach or kale, finely chopped (optional)

¼ cup Homemade Vegan Mayo (page 196) or store-bought vegan mayo

2 tablespoons relish or diced pickles

2 tablespoons finely diced onion

2 tablespoons freshly squeezed lemon juice

¼ teaspoon fine sea salt

Pinch or two of freshly ground black pepper

Tabasco hot sauce, for serving (I love the smoked chipotle kind!)

Potato chips, for serving

First, drain the chickpeas (see Save the Bean Juice! below for what to do with the liquid) and put them in a smallish bowl. Mash with a fork until most of the beans are flattened. (This actually takes a little strength—the beans can be tough. I often smash them against the side of the bowl, or you can try a plate.) Add the spinach (if using) the mayo, relish, onion, lemon juice, salt, and pepper and stir to combine. Add more relish to taste if needed. Serve with hot sauce and potato chips. Use immediately or store in the fridge for up to 3 days.

☆ Save the Bean Juice!

Also known as aquafaba, the starchy liquid in a can of chickpeas is magical! It can whip up into a meringue and is a great vegan replacement for eggs. Not all chickpea juices are created equal, though. The liquid from canned chickpeas usually works better than that from home cooked. Try using aquafaba in Five-Ingredient Crepes (page 91).

RICE PAPER
Bacon
SNACK STRIPS

Rice paper is great because it absorbs the flavor of whatever it's soaked in (soy sauce in this case), and the edges get crispy when it's baked, like bacon. It's sweet, chewy, gives an umami hit, and oh, it is good.

Makes
12 BACON STRIPS

Cooking spray

3½ ounces (¼ of a standard package) firm tofu, drained

3 to 4 baby bella mushrooms, or 1 portobello mushroom cap

¼ cup soy sauce

2 tablespoons maple syrup

4 rice paper sheets

¼ cup Soy Sauce Syrup (page 193)

2 tablespoons extra-virgin olive oil

½ teaspoon freshly ground black pepper

¼ teaspoon cayenne pepper

1 Preheat the oven to 400°F. Coat a sheet pan with cooking spray. Set aside.

2 Add the tofu, baby bella mushrooms, 2 tablespoons of the soy sauce, and the maple syrup to a blender and pulse until a paste forms.

3 Pour the remaining 2 tablespoons soy sauce into a wide, shallow bowl. Soak one sheet of rice paper in the sauce for 5 seconds, remove, and lay flat on a cutting board or sheet pan. Spread half of the tofu-mushroom paste, about ½ cup, evenly over the rice paper. Repeat the soaking process with a second sheet and lay it on top of the first rice paper sheet to evenly cover.

4 Using kitchen shears, slice the mushroom-filled rice paper "sandwich" into 6 strips. Place the strips on the prepared sheet pan at least 1 inch apart. Repeat the entire process with the remaining two rice paper sheets to make 6 more strips. In a small bowl, stir together the Soy Sauce Syrup, olive oil, and black and cayenne peppers. Brush the mixture on the 12 strips.

5 Bake until the rice paper bubbles and browns at the edges, 15 to 20 minutes. Let the strips cool on the sheet pan for 10 minutes before eating. Enjoy immediately or wrap in a paper towel and in an airtight bag or container for up to 2 days.

SOFT
CENTER

Kale PUFFS

These are my vegan take on gougères, those savory French cheese puffs made from an eggy choux pastry dough, which I didn't know anything about until I watched *The Great British Bake Off*. Leftover rice, when whipped up, becomes an incredible chewy eggless dough that puffs when baked. The outside of these delectable puffs is crunchy, and the inside is almost creamy, like risotto. I save my rice bags and use them as piping bags, or you can use a mini ice cream scoop if you don't have a bag. A teaspoon works, too. This recipe is a good way to finish off a bag of greens, stems and all.

Makes
ABOUT 15 TO 20 PUFFS

1 cup One Week's Worth of Sushi Rice (page 186) or leftover rice

1 cup firmly packed bagged kale or spinach

1 tablespoon nutritional yeast

2 teaspoons white vinegar

2 teaspoons extra-virgin olive oil or avocado oil

1 teaspoon garlic powder

1 teaspoon dried parsley

½ teaspoon fine sea salt, plus more for sprinkling

1 Preheat the oven to 425°F. Line a sheet pan with parchment paper. Set aside.

2 First, warm the rice. Put it in a microwave-safe bowl, sprinkle it lightly with water, and heat it in the microwave for a minute or two. Don't have one? Warm the leftover rice on the stovetop in a skillet with some water.

3 Next, combine the warmed rice, spinach, nutritional yeast, vinegar, olive oil, garlic powder, parsley, and salt in a blender or food processor and run on high until the mixture is well combined and mostly smooth and elastic, scraping down the sides of the blender or bowl as needed. It should be a little sticky, like a choux dough.

4 Transfer the rice dough to a piping bag and form 1-inch circles placed at least 2 inches apart on the prepared sheet pan (or you can also use a teaspoon and scoop the dough).

5 Bake until puffed and shiny, 15 to 20 minutes. You should be able to tap them and they will sound almost hollow. Sprinkle with more salt and serve immediately (they are best eaten right away).

CHIPS, CHIPS, 'SALSA', and MORE

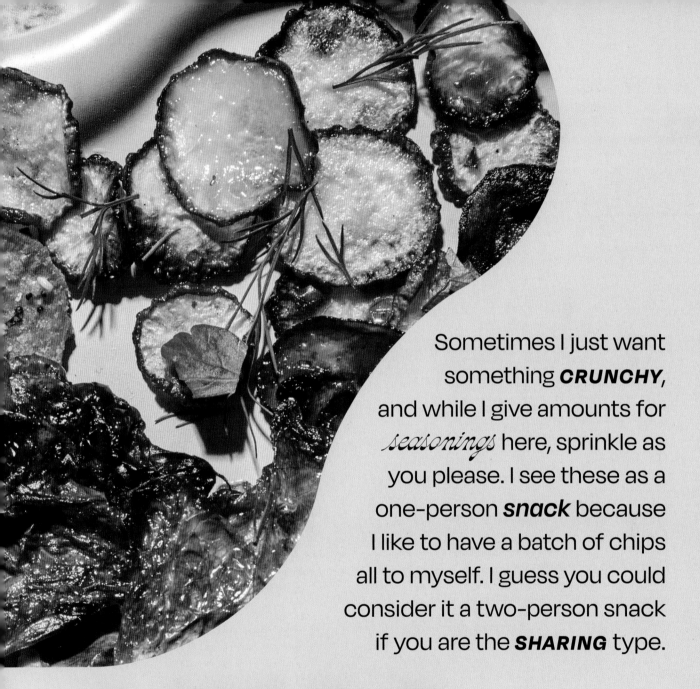

Sometimes I just want something **CRUNCHY**, and while I give amounts for *seasonings* here, sprinkle as you please. I see these as a one-person **snack** because I like to have a batch of chips all to myself. I guess you could consider it a two-person snack if you are the **SHARING** type.

CHIPS

Cabbage Leaf Chips

SERVES 1

8 to 10 green cabbage leaves, torn in half (red works, too)

3 tablespoons extra-virgin olive oil

¼ teaspoon ground cumin

⅛ teaspoon fine sea salt

Pinch or two of freshly ground black pepper

Preheat the oven to 400°F.

Place the leaves in a large bowl. Drizzle with the olive oil, and using your hands, massage it evenly over all the leaves. Sprinkle with the cumin, salt, and pepper and toss to coat.

Spread the leaves in a single layer on a sheet pan.

Bake until the leaves are crisped through, about 15 minutes. Let cool before enjoying.

Sweet Potato Chips

SERVES 1

Delicious with Pickle Guac (page 129)

1 large sweet potato, peeled and cut into ⅛-inch rounds

1 tablespoon extra-virgin olive oil

2 to 3 tablespoons Hal's Everything Seasoning (page 187) or your favorite seasoning mix

Fine sea salt, for serving

Preheat the oven to 425°F.

Place the potato rounds into a medium bowl, drizzle with the olive oil, and toss to coat. Sprinkle with Hal's seasoning and toss again. Spread the rounds in a single layer on a sheet pan. Bake for 10 minutes, flip, then bake until golden and cooked through, another 10 to 15 minutes. Sprinkle with salt before serving.

Crispy Radish Coins

SERVES 1

1 bunch radishes (about 10), ends removed and cut into ⅛-inch rounds

2 tablespoons extra-virgin olive oil

1 tablespoon white vinegar

2 tablespoons dried dill

¼ teaspoon fine sea salt

2 pinches of white pepper

Preheat the oven to 425°F.

Place the radish rounds into a medium bowl, drizzle with the olive oil and vinegar, and toss to coat. Sprinkle with the dill, salt, and white pepper and toss again. Spread the rounds in a single layer on a sheet pan. Bake for 10 minutes, flip, and bake for another 10 to 15 minutes until golden. Serve immediately.

Crunchy Mushroom Crisps

SERVES 1

8 ounces baby bella mushrooms, cut into ⅛-inch slices

1 tablespoon extra-virgin olive oil

1 tablespoon Balsamic Glaze (page 191) or store-bought

¼ teaspoon fine sea salt, plus more for serving

¼ teaspoon freshly ground black pepper

Dried parsley, for serving

Preheat the oven to 375°F.

Spread the mushrooms on a sheet pan, drizzle with the olive oil and the Balsamic Glaze, and toss to coat. Sprinkle with the salt and pepper and toss again. Spread the mushrooms in a single layer on the sheet pan. Bake in the oven for 10 minutes. Then flip the mushrooms and continue baking until crispy golden, another 10 to 15 minutes. Be sure to cook until they are crispy, as they won't continue to crisp once out of the oven. Let cool. To serve, sprinkle with parsley and a pinch of salt.

Let the mushroom crisps cool before eating. They are always best eaten right away!

Cucumber BITES

Crisp and fresh, these cucumber bites give me the feeling I'm eating an inverted Japanese-style cucumber roll. It's a fun way to eat a bunch of different veggies in one bite (BYOR—Build Your Own Roll). And the roll is great to travel with whole, so you can cut it right before serving. I like to lightly peel my cucumbers to create a striped effect, both for the visual appeal and for the taste and texture, as peeling reduces some of the bitterness and the toughness—large cukes or ones from the garden can have quite tough peels.

Makes
6 TO 8 BITES

1 medium cucumber, with stripes of peel removed (see headnote)

¼ cup One Week's Worth of Sushi Rice (page 186)

¼ peeled and thinly sliced avocado, and/or 1 handful of any combination of the following:
½ thinly sliced bell pepper,
½ julienned small carrot,
1 thinly sliced green onion

Sprinkle of fine sea salt

Sesame seeds, for serving

2 tablespoons Ranchy Dressing (page 192) or soy sauce, for serving

1 Slice off both ends of the cucumber, and using a metal straw (or very stiff plastic one), pierce through the center of one end of the cucumber and push the straw through to the opposite side, removing the seeds as you push. A chopstick or small paring knife works well for this job, too. Continue to pierce through the original hole, cleaning out the cuke center, until the opening is ¾-inch wide. To make cleaning easier, you can cut the cucumber in half so you have two tubes instead of one.

2 Hold the cucumber vertically on a flat surface, and using the straw or a chopstick if needed, stuff half of the empty space with rice and avocado, then stuff the cucumber with any vegetables you are using. There is no wrong way here. Just try to pack in as much rice and as many vegetables into the cuke tube as possible. Slice the stuffed cucumber horizontally into 6 to 8 rounds (like a sushi roll).

3 Sprinkle the bites with salt and sesame seeds. Serve immediately with the Ranchy Dressing for dipping.

☆ Make It Hearty
Add savory fillings of your choice, like thinly sliced Air-Fryer Smoky Tofu Tips (page 124), seasoned mashed chickpeas, or Lentil Ground Beef (page 104) for a more protein-packed bite.

ANGRY.

When eating these umami **CHILI** *snacks* I recommend biting into the shell so you get a hit of the spicy sauce alongside the **sweetness** of the little green beans inside (as opposed to shelling them in your hand). These bean *bombs* are downright addictive. And oh so easy to make. The technique of **mixing** the sauce in the bag makes for fewer dishes and less mess. Even better.

Edamame

Makes
ABOUT 4 CUPS

**1 (14-ounce) bag frozen unshelled
edamame or snap peas**

For the Angry Sauce
2 tablespoons soy sauce

1 tablespoon organic light brown sugar

1 tablespoon extra-virgin olive oil

2 teaspoons red pepper flakes

1 teaspoon sesame oil

**1 teaspoon minced garlic
(1 to 2 small cloves)**

1 teaspoon sesame seeds

Pinch of fine sea salt

1   Steam the edamame in the microwave according to the package
instructions (save the bag, you'll need it in a bit). Or you can cook
them on the stovetop: place a steamer basket over a pot filled with
1 inch of water. Once the water is boiling, add the frozen edamame to the
basket. Cover and steam for 3 to 5 minutes. Then remove from the heat
and return them to the original package.

2   *Next, make the Angry Sauce:* In a small microwave-safe bowl,
combine the soy sauce, brown sugar, olive oil, pepper flakes,
sesame oil, and garlic. Microwave on high for 15 seconds until the
sugar has dissolved. Again, you may also heat this sauce on the stovetop.

3   Once the edamame have cooled, pour the Angry Sauce into the bag
and shake to coat. Pour the coated beans into a serving dish.
Sprinkle them with sesame seeds and salt.

4   Store in an airtight container and enjoy for up to 2 days. These are
just as tasty right out of the fridge as when you first make them!

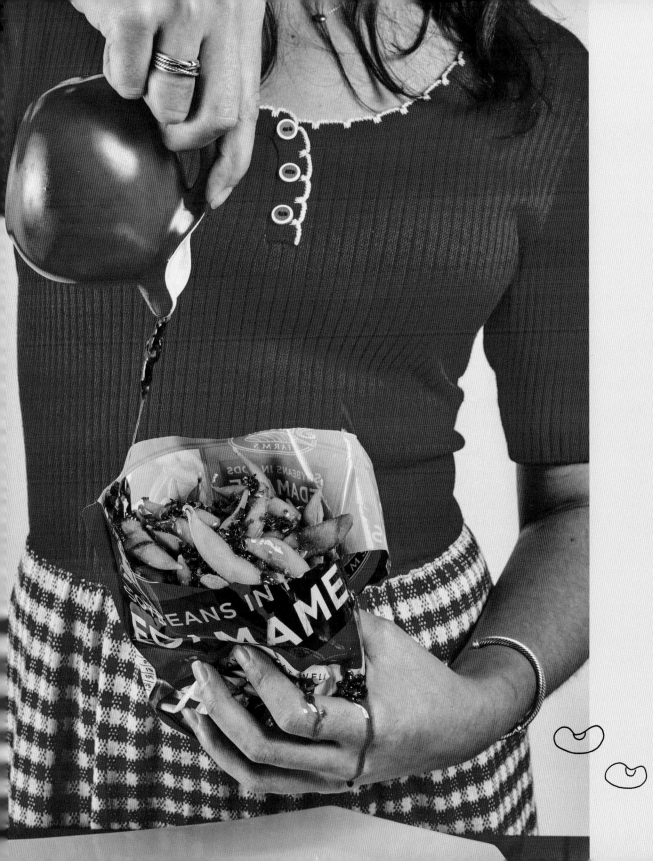

41

If Uncrustables were an appetizer, they would look like these bite-size sandwich pockets. This snack is a great way to use up old bread, and you can use any left-over crusts for bread crumbs. A word about the bread: don't get too fancy. Good old school-lunch sandwich bread is what you need here—you know, the kind that is soft enough to hold a thumbprint. When I fill these pockets with something savory, I like to sprinkle a little seasoning on top before baking.

Makes
3 POCKETS

6 slices soft multigrain sandwich bread

6 tablespoons filling of choice, such as Mixed Berry Chia Jam (page 223), Chocolate Protein Spread (209), Trail Mix Butter (page 210), or Kale Pesto Crumble (page 224)

Cooking spray

1   Preheat the oven or air fryer to 375°F.

2   Lay out 3 slices of bread and spread each one generously with 2 tablespoons of your filling of choice. Top each slice with a remaining slice of bread.

3   Using a cup or a lid or a round biscuit cutter, 1½ to 2 inches in diameter, cut rounds from each sandwich. Pinch the edges of each round until they are sealed. Coat each pocket lightly with cooking spray and place them on a sheet pan.

4   Bake or air-fry until golden, 5 to 8 minutes. Serve immediately.

TOASTY *Sandwich* POCKETS

Potato Peel CRUNCHES

I make these with both fresh peels and leftover peels from steamed potatoes (see Potato Cheese, page 204), just not at the same time, as the cooking time differs slightly. Crisping up this nutrient-packed potato part is just one example of how easy it is to make food waste into a snackable crunch. They're also great for dipping. Try them with my Spicy Mayo (page 197).

Serves
1 TO 2

Peels from two large raw, washed potatoes (russet, Yukon Gold, or any larger potato variety will work)

2 teaspoons extra-virgin olive oil

¼ teaspoon garlic powder

¼ teaspoon onion powder

¼ teaspoon dried parsley

Pinch of fine sea salt

1 Preheat the oven to 400°F.

 2 If using fresh peels, pat them dry with a paper towel. If using peeled skins from steamed potatoes, you may want to cut them into thin slices like you'd get from a potato peeler.

 3 Put the skins on a sheet pan, drizzle with the olive oil, and toss to coat. Next, sprinkle the skins with the garlic and onion powders, parsley, and salt. Toss again to distribute the spices evenly.

 4 Lay the peels flat and in a single layer on the same sheet pan, and bake until they are golden and crispy, about 10 minutes for peels from steamed potatoes and 15 minutes for fresh peels. Remove from the oven and let cool before enjoying. Store in an airtight container for up to 3 days.

MOON Cheeze

This salty, crunchy snack is a copy of an American staple. It takes about an hour, and the results are incredible, and honestly, more flavorful than the original Cheez-It. After it's left out to dry for a bit, the cheese gets extra crispy and light in the oven. One of my favorite vegan cheeses is by Chao, but this method works with essentially any brand of vegan sliced cheese. I can picture it on a charcuterie board, as a salad topping, or served with a side of Pickle Guac (page 129), but honestly, it's hard not to eat them right off the sheet pan straight from the oven.

1 HEAPING CUP

6 vegan cheese slices

Hal's Everything Seasoning (page 187) or dried herbs, for serving

 Stack 6 vegan cheese slices on a cutting board and cut the stack into thirds vertically and then thirds horizontally to get 9 equal squares, which will yield 54 (1-to-1½-inch) total squares. Arrange the squares on a sheet pan in a single layer. Cover loosely with a paper towel and let air-dry on the counter for 1 hour.

2 Preheat the oven to 375°F.

3 Uncover the dried cheese and bake until golden and crispy like a cracker, about 15 minutes. Enjoy as is, or with a sprinkle of Hal's seasoning. These can be stored in a jar or airtight container for up to 5 days.

Avocadough CRACKERS

Do you have an extra half of an avocado? This quick and easy snack is a great way to use it up, or go ahead and make these solely for the purpose of creating a delicious lime-green batch of gluten-free wafer-thin crackers. I like to use a pizza cutter and slice my dough directly on the pan so I can break it apart once it's baked. With a little flaky salt, this snack has a mild, ripe avocado flavor and great crunch.

Makes
12 TO 20 CRACKERS,
depending on how you cut them

1 batch GF Avocadough (page 217), plus extra gluten-free flour for rolling out

1 tablespoon extra-virgin olive oil

Flaky sea salt

Toppings such as 1 tablespoon black sesame seeds, poppy seeds, etc. (optional)

1 Preheat the oven to 450°F.

2 Lay a piece of parchment paper the size of your sheet pan on a work surface. Sprinkle the parchment with flour and place the avocadough on the paper.

3 Using a rolling pin or glass bottle, roll out the avocadough in a circle (about 10 inches in diameter) as thin as you can get it, about ⅛ inch thick. Transfer the parchment with the rolled dough to a sheet pan.

4 Brush the dough with the olive oil, and using a pizza cutter, cut the dough into your desired cracker shapes. Sprinkle with flaky sea salt and any toppings you may be using. You may need to press seeds into the dough to get them to stick.

5 Bake until the crackers start to turn golden on the edges and feel crispy, 15 to 18 minutes. Since the crackers on the outside tend to bake faster, you can remove the crackers on the edge using a spatula and continue cooking the crackers near the center until they get crispier. Transfer the crackers to a wire rack and allow them to cool completely before eating (they'll continue to crisp up). Store in an airtight container for up to 3 days.

TWO-INGREDIENT

Pretzel CLOUD BITES

These pretzels are just perfect in my opinion, thanks to the pillowy dough that gives them a light and chewy bite. Interestingly, they stay white like a cloud as they bake, yet they have a classic pretzel flavor thanks to the baking soda bath. I like to keep an eye on the bottoms of the bites as they cook—once they're golden, they're ready.

Makes

ABOUT 18 BITES

½ cup self-rising flour, plus more for rolling out

⅓ cup plus 1 tablespoon unsweetened soy-based yogurt, such as Silk

1 tablespoon baking soda

2 tablespoons vegan butter, melted

Sea salt, for sprinkling

¼ cup finely chopped almonds and/or 2 tablespoons cinnamon sugar, for topping (optional)

 Preheat the oven to 400°F. Line a sheet pan with parchment paper. Set aside.

 In a medium bowl, stir the flour and yogurt to form a pillowy dough. It will be quite sticky. Flour your fingers and divide the dough ball into two rounds.

 Put one of the dough rounds onto a generously floured surface (use at least 1 to 2 tablespoons of flour), and using a very light touch, roll it into a thin snake shape, about 1 inch in diameter and 9 inches long. Using a knife or bench scraper, cut the dough snake into bite-size pieces, about the length of a paper clip (1 inch each). Again, the dough is soft and pillowy, so keep a light touch. Repeat the rolling-out process with the second dough round.

 Next, fill a medium saucepot half full with water and bring it to a boil. Turn down the heat and add the baking soda, which will dissolve immediately. Keep the heat on low so the water is gently simmering, and submerge the dough bites for 20 seconds. I like to cook these a few at a time, using a fork to add them to and remove them from the baking soda water.

 Place the boiled bites on the prepared sheet pan and bake until golden brown on the bottom, about 18 minutes.

 After the pretzel bites are baked, dip their tops in the melted butter and sprinkle with salt, and if using, finely chopped almonds and/or cinnamon and sugar. While these are best eaten right away, they can be stored in an airtight container for up to 2 days.

☆ No Self-Rising Flour? Make Your Own!

Combine ½ cup all-purpose flour with ½ teaspoon baking powder, ¼ teaspoon salt, and ⅛ teaspoon baking soda.

BABY

Although carrot fries are good in theory, I often find them limp and sad. Thanks to a coating of starch, these carrot fries have a **CRISPY-ISH** exterior and yet maintain the soft, *subtle* sweet goodness of a cooked carrot inside. Be sure to use baby or petite carrots for this recipe. Cut carrots will not hold their shape. The spice gives them a nice **SMOKY** flavor, too. And the *sauce*—don't get me started. The tangy, spicy, and *sweet* blend of lemon juice, sriracha, and maple in a vegan mayo makes for the best flavor combination ever.

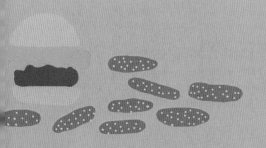

CARR

Serves
2 TO 4

1 (12-ounce) bag baby or petite carrots

1 tablespoon extra-virgin olive oil

2 tablespoons all-purpose flour

2 tablespoons Hal's Everything Seasoning (page 187) or vegan seasoned bread crumbs

1 tablespoon tapioca starch

1 teaspoon smoked paprika

1 teaspoon ground cumin

Cooking spray

Finely chopped fresh parsley (optional)

Fine sea salt, for extra seasoning (optional)

For the sauce

1 tablespoon Homemade Vegan Mayo (page 196) or store-bought vegan mayo

1 teaspoon freshly squeezed lemon juice or white vinegar

1 teaspoon sriracha

1 teaspoon maple syrup

1 Preheat the oven to 425°F. Line a sheet pan with parchment paper. Set aside.

2 Put the carrots into a medium bowl. Drizzle with the olive oil and toss. In another bowl, combine the flour, Hal's seasoning, tapioca starch, paprika, and cumin. Sprinkle this dry mix onto the carrots and toss again until evenly coated.

3 Spread the carrots in a single layer on the prepared sheet pan so they are not touching each other, and spray with cooking spray for a golden crust.

4 Bake for 10 to 12 minutes. Then shake the pan, and using tongs or a spatula, turn the carrrots. Continue to bake until they just start to darken on the edges, turn somewhat crisp, and are easy to pierce with a fork, around 10 minutes.

5 *Meanwhile, make the sauce:* In a small bowl stir together the mayo, lemon juice, sriracha, and maple syrup.

6 Serve the carrot fries with a sprinkle of parsley and salt (if using) and the sauce.

Crispy Sprout Skins

SERVES 1 TO 2

½ pound (12 large or 20 small) Brussels sprouts

1 tablespoon extra-virgin olive oil

½ teaspoon fine sea salt

Freshly ground black pepper

Preheat the oven to 400°F.

Cut the ends off each sprout. Preserve any leaves that fall, and begin to peel the sprout, leaf by leaf. When you can't peel off any more leaves, cut the remaining sprout into thin slices.

Spread the sprout leaves and slices on a sheet pan. Toss with the olive oil and sprinkle with the salt and a few pinches of pepper. Bake for 10 minutes, toss, then continue to bake, checking at 5-minute intervals, until the leaves are golden and crisp. Let cool before enjoying.

Smashed Sprouts

SERVES 2 TO 4

1 pound (about 24 large or 40 small) steamed Brussels sprouts, patted dry

2 tablespoons extra-virgin olive oil

½ teaspoon fine sea salt

⅛ teaspoon freshly ground black pepper

3 to 4 tablespoons Spicy Citrus Vinaigrette (page 190) or Angry Sauce (page 40)

Preheat the oven to 425°F.

Put the steamed sprouts on a sheet pan, and using the bottom of a cup, flatten each sprout until it's about ¼ inch thick. Then drizzle with the olive oil, sprinkle with the salt and pepper, and very gently toss to coat. Spread out the sprouts, leaving an inch or so between each one (you may need two sheet pans), and bake until deep golden brown (the edges should be almost charred) and crispy, 25 to 30 minutes, flipping once about halfway through the cooking time. Drizzle with the vinaigrette, toss to coat, and serve.

Brussels sprouts are one of my favorite under-dog vegetables. I'm convinced that everything is better when it's a little bit crispy, and all three of these recipes show just how pretty and versatile these baby cabbages are.

Sprouted Brussels

SERVES 1 TO 2

½ pound (12 large or 20 small) steamed Brussels sprouts, patted dry

2 tablespoons extra-virgin olive oil

½ teaspoon fine sea salt

Hal's Everything Sauce (page 189), for serving

Preheat the oven to 425°F.

In a medium bowl, toss the steamed sprouts in the olive oil and salt.

Slice each sprout in half, two-thirds of the way through, and again in the opposite direction to make a plus sign. Gently peel back the individual leaves from each wedge to create a flower shape. Put the sprouts on a sheet pan and bake until the centers of the sprouts start to turn gold and the edges of the flowers crisp some, 15 to 20 minutes. Drizzle with the sauce to serve.

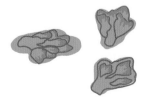

THREE WAYS TO STEAM BRUSSELS SPROUTS

1 **Microwave:** Put the sprouts into a microwave-safe dish with 1 tablespoon of water and cook on high for 1 minute. Continue cooking, checking at 30-second intervals until the sprouts reach your desired tenderness.

2 **Stovetop Steamer:** Put the sprouts into a pan fitted with a steamer basket and about 1 inch of water. Bring the water to a boil, place a lid on top of the pan, and steam until the sprouts reach your desired tenderness, about 8 minutes.

3 **Stovetop Skillet:** Put the sprouts into a skillet with about ½ to 1 inch of water. Over medium heat, bring the water to a simmer. Cover and cook until the sprouts reach your desired tenderness, about 5 minutes.

Protein

BARS

This is my take on Perfect Bars, those popular refrigerated peanut butter snacks. There's just something about putting a nut butter protein bar in the fridge that makes the texture so much better—the consistency becomes almost fudge-like. They have the crunch of puffed rice and whatever seeds or nuts you use. I especially like adding chia seeds. These are essentially a combination of all my favorite toppings and are a good way to use up what's left in bags of seeds or nuts. Instead of pressing the dough into a pan, I just press the dough with parchment, creating a protein slab that I cut into bars. For a more uniform shape, you can roll this dough into balls, too.

Makes
ABOUT 10 BARS

1 cup natural nut butter (see About Nut Butters, below)—I like cashew or peanut butter

½ cup puffed rice cereal

¼ cup nuts or seeds, like chia seeds, sunflower seeds, finely chopped pecans, etc.

2 tablespoons of your favorite unflavored or vanilla vegan protein powder

3 to 4 tablespoons Cheap & Sweet Syrup (page 194) or maple syrup

¼ cup mini vegan chocolate chips

1 In a blender or food processor, combine the nut butter, puffed rice cereal, the nuts or seeds you are using, and the protein powder. Pulse until a rough dough forms.

2 Add the Cheap & Sweet Syrup 1 tablespoon at a time, scraping the sides after each addition, and continue to pulse until the dough pulls away from the sides of the blender or food processor bowl.

3 Lay a piece of parchment paper on a sheet pan and place the dough in the center of the paper. Cover it with a second piece of parchment. Using your fingers, press the dough out into a flat 6-inch-square slab that's about ¾ inch thick. Pull back the parchment and sprinkle the chocolate chips in an even layer over the slab and press them into the dough. Cover with plastic wrap and chill the dough for at least 1 hour. (You can definitely eat them right away, but the texture improves as they chill.)

4 Slice into 10 bars. Store in an airtight container in the fridge or freezer for up to 2 weeks.

☆ About Nut Butters

It is important to use natural nut butter for these bars, otherwise they won't set. Non-natural nut butters often have additives like palm oil that keep them soft and spreadable, which means even in the fridge, these bars won't stiffen up.

CINNAMON GRANOLA *Bark*

Makes
ABOUT 5 CUPS

1 cup whole raw almonds

½ cup whole raw pecans

½ cup dried fruit, such as cranberries or figs

2 cups DIY Oat Flour (page 215) or store-bought oat flour

½ cup pumpkin or sunflower seeds

¼ cup chia seeds or flaxseed

1 teaspoon ground cinnamon

½ teaspoon ground nutmeg

½ teaspoon fine sea salt

¼ cup extra-virgin olive oil or refined coconut oil, melted

¼ cup Cheap & Sweet Syrup (page 194) or maple syrup

2 tablespoons unsweetened almond or oat milk

½ teaspoon pure vanilla extract

Packed with so many good things, this granola bark has everything in every bite.

1. Preheat the oven to 325°F. Line a sheet pan with parchment paper. Set aside.

2. Chop the almonds, pecans, and dried fruit until pebble-like, to retain some chunks and texture.

3. Place the chopped ingredients into a large bowl and add the DIY Oat Flour, pumpkin seeds, chia seeds, cinnamon, nutmeg, and salt; stir to combine. Next pour in the olive oil, Cheap & Sweet Syrup, almond milk, and vanilla. Toss until well combined and all the dry bits are moistened.

4. Transfer the mixture to the prepared sheet pan and form a rectangle about ½ inch thick, pressing firmly to eliminate any spaces in the mixture.

5. Bake for 20 minutes. Then to ensure even baking, rotate the pan 180 degrees and continue to bake until fragrant and golden, 15 to 20 more minutes.

6. Remove from the oven and allow the granola to cool completely in the pan. The granola rectangle will harden as it cools, so resist any temptation to move it. Once it is cool, break it into bark-like pieces and use as a topping on yogurt or store in an airtight container for later. (It will keep for at least a week—that is, if it lasts that long!)

2. BEFO

ORE

Noon

Fluffy

Vegan OMELET

I WAS INTRODUCED TO THIS LENTIL RECIPE WHILE STUDYING AT A VEGAN CULINARY SCHOOL IN INDIA. ONE MORNING THE HEAD CHEF MADE US A FLUFFY SLICED SNACK FROM SOAKED LENTILS, AND THE TEXTURE REMINDED ME OF AN OMELET, SO HERE IT IS: SOAKED LENTILS TURNED OMELET WITH MY OWN SPIN. IT'S PACKED WITH PROTEIN, FLAVOR, AND EGG-PLUS-INDIAN-RELATED NOSTALGIA.

2 OMELETS

For the "egg" batter

1 cup split yellow mung beans (moong dal), soaked in water to cover overnight

½ cup plus 2 tablespoons unsweetened almond milk

1 teaspoon freshly squeezed lemon juice

½ teaspoon fine sea salt or black salt (for more about black salt, see page 63)

¼ teaspoon chili powder

¼ teaspoon baking powder

⅛ teaspoon turmeric, for color

⅛ teaspoon freshly ground black pepper

For the omelet

1 to 2 tablespoons extra-virgin olive oil or vegan butter

Handful of bagged spinach leaves

2 tablespoons shredded vegan cheddar

Sriracha, for serving

1 *First, make the "egg" batter:* Drain the beans, rinse, and drain again (you should have a generous 2¼ cups soaked beans). Add the drained beans to the blender and pulse until roughly chopped. Add the almond milk, lemon juice, sea salt, chili powder, baking powder, turmeric, and pepper. Blend until a thick, smooth paste forms.

2 *Next, make the omelet:* In a medium nonstick skillet over medium heat, warm 1 tablespoon of the olive oil until it shimmers. Using a spatula, scrape half of the bean mixture from the blender into the skillet and spread it out into a thin, even round that fills the pan, or to the desired thickness. Place half the spinach and shredded cheddar on half of the round and reduce the heat to low. Cook until the mixture starts to bubble as a pancake would, and the edges are set, about 2 minutes. With a silicone spatula, loosen the plain side of the omelet and lift the edge to fold it in half. Cook until the bottom is golden and the batter is cooked through, another 2 minutes or so. (If the middle is not yet set, flip the omelet over again, keeping the heat very low, and continue to cook for a few more minutes, until the center is cooked through.) Repeat the process for the second omelet. Serve immediately.

 ## Scramble Me, Please

In a medium skillet over medium-low heat, warm the olive oil or vegan butter until it shimmers or melts. Pour ⅓ to ½ cup yellow mung bean mixture from the recipe above into a skillet and spread it out in a ½-inch layer. Cook for a minute or two. Then drag a spatula through the mixture, and toss and scramble to break up the batter. Continue to stir and cook until the desired "dryness" is achieved, about 4 minutes for a medium-dry scramble.

·A· *Breakfast* SANDWICH

(MAKE YOUR OWN BREAD)

If you're going to make your own bread, you might as well re-create a vegan egg to complete this creamy, fluffy breakfast sandwich. Made accidentally while we were photographing this book, the fluke resulted in a creation worth its own page. Using the "egg" batter from my Fluffy Vegan Omelet (page 60), this smaller omelet is the perfect portion of vegan egg in my homemade roll. I like to use black salt to imitate the yolky umami flavor of eggs so you won't be missing anything when you take your first bite (and every other bite after that).

Serves

1

1 Emergency Bread roll
(page 221)

1 to 2 teaspoons vegan butter

2 teaspoons extra-virgin
olive oil

¼ cup "egg" batter (see Fluffy
Vegan Omelet, page 60)

5 to 6 baby spinach leaves

1 tablespoon shredded vegan
cheddar

Sriracha, for serving (optional)

 First, cut the roll in half, toast it, and spread it with the butter.

 Next, in a small nonstick skillet over medium heat, warm the olive oil until it shimmers. Using a ¼ cup measure, pour the "egg" batter into the skillet and spread it out into a thin, even 4-inch round, or to the desired thickness. Place the spinach and shredded cheddar on half of the round and reduce the heat to low. Cook until the mixture starts to bubble as a pancake would, and the edges are set, about 2 minutes. With a silicone spatula, loosen the plain side of the mini omelet and lift the edge to fold it in half. Cook until the bottom is golden and the batter is cooked through, another 2 minutes or so.

 Place the mini omelet on the bottom half of the roll, add sriracha, if using, and finish the sandwich with the roll top. Serve immediately.

What Exactly Is Black Salt?

Himalayan black salt, also called kala namak, was something I learned about at culinary school in India. The raw material for the compound originally came from mines in India and the Himalayas. It has a sulfurous smell and flavor, which makes it great for vegan egg recipes. You can usually find it in Asian grocery stores, and it is easily available online.

Cinnamon

Tortillas are a pantry staple for me. When I'm not making them, I'm making things with them, like this wrap bowl, which is a wonderful edible vessel for yogurt *and* kind of tastes like a churro. It can easily be made savory with a few adjustments (see Make It Savory!), and it's a fun way to use up any leftover wraps in your pantry.

Serves
1

1 (8-inch) flour tortilla

2 teaspoons vegan butter or refined coconut oil

1 teaspoon cane sugar

¼ teaspoon ground cinnamon

½ to ¾ cup of your favorite vegan yogurt

Spoonful of Trail Mix Butter (page 210) or store-bought nut butter

Blueberries and walnuts, for topping

 Preheat the oven to 400°F.

 Lay the tortilla flat and spread the vegan butter evenly over one side of it, covering the entire surface. Then sprinkle it all over with the sugar and cinnamon.

 Put the tortilla, butter and cinnamon side out, in an oven-safe bowl or ramekin about 5 inches in diameter and 2 inches high and form it into a bowl shape. (The tortilla will fold over itself a little, almost like a pleat, to form a round, which is okay.) Bake until crispy and the edges turn golden, 15 to 18 minutes.

 When the wrap bowl is cooled, remove it from the dish and fill with the yogurt. Top with a dollop of Trail Mix Butter, and sprinkle with blueberries and walnuts.

☆ Make It Savory!
For a savory breakfast bowl, swap out the cinnamon sugar for a light sprinkling of salt and paprika, and bake as directed above. Fill the baked shell with vegan scrambled eggs (see Scramble Me, Please, page 61) and top with chopped fresh herbs.

Sugar Tortilla Bowl

Chocolate Shell SMOOTHIE 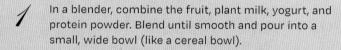 BOWL

Serves
1

1 cup frozen fruit of choice

¼ cup Instant Plant Milk (page 199) or unsweetened oat milk

2 tablespoons vegan yogurt of choice

2 tablespoons of your favorite unflavored or vanilla vegan protein powder

For the Chocolate Shell

2 tablespoons refined coconut oil, melted

1 tablespoon unsweetened cocoa powder

1 teaspoon maple syrup or sweetener of choice

This recipe is as fun to make as it is to eat—there's something very satisfying about cracking that shell! The coconut oil in the topping dries instantly when you pour it over the cold smoothie base. You can watch it "magically" harden before your eyes. Plus it adds some delectable crunch and cocoa flavor to your morning bowl.

1. In a blender, combine the fruit, plant milk, yogurt, and protein powder. Blend until smooth and pour into a small, wide bowl (like a cereal bowl).

2. *Make the Chocolate Shell:* In a second small bowl, stir together the coconut oil, cocoa powder, and maple syrup until smooth.

3. Pour the chocolate mixture in an even layer over the smoothie bowl, twisting and turning the bowl to evenly spread out the topping. The chocolate will harden after about 5 minutes. If you want to speed up the process or if it doesn't harden completely, you can put it in the freezer for a few minutes. Crack with a spoon and enjoy!

Serves

1

1 tablespoon creamy or crunchy peanut butter

1 store-bought 6- or 8-ounce vegan yogurt cup

1 tablespoon Mixed Berry Chia Jam (page 223) or jam of choice

1 recipe Chocolate Shell (page 66)

This is a three-layer breakfast cup that gets better with every bite. Think of Talenti Gelato Layers, only twice as creamy and half the cost. The tart jam, the nutty peanut butter crunch, and the chocolate chunks that form as you dig into the top shell make for a satisfying morning bite (or dessert for breakfast). No matter what time of day you decide to pull your cup out of the freezer, this recipe is a gem.

Stir the peanut butter into the yogurt cup. Then dollop the Mixed Berry Chia Jam in the center and push it down to cover with the yogurt. Pour the Chocolate Shell in an even layer over the yogurt to completely cover. (You'll get a nice thick layer of chocolate—the smaller the container, the thicker the chocolate.) Freeze for at least 30 minutes before enjoying.

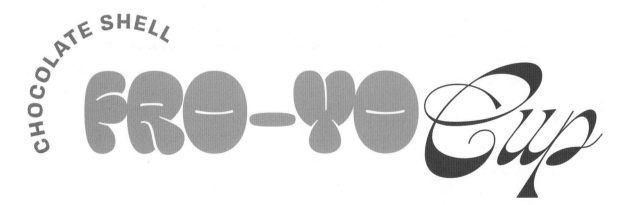

CHOCOLATE SHELL FRO-YO Cup

CHUNKY COCOA-BANANA
Stovetop GRANOLA

Granola is a snack I want available at all times, and in a perfect world, it would always be on hand. However, sometimes preheating the oven is just one step too many, so behold this stovetop wonder. I can live out my granola morning dreams with minimal effort. I like to eat it as a cereal or sprinkle it on top of a breakfast bowl. You can also use it for a cookie mix-in. We're getting creative.

Makes
A GENEROUS 1½ CUPS

1 ripe banana, peeled

1½ cups old-fashioned rolled oats

2 tablespoons organic cane sugar

2 tablespoons unsweetened cocoa powder

1 tablespoon all-purpose flour

1 teaspoon pure vanilla extract

Pinch of fine sea salt

1 In a large bowl, mash the banana. Add the oats, sugar, cocoa powder, flour, vanilla, and salt, and using a fork, continue to mash and stir, working the ingredients together until fully combined.

2 Put the mixture in a large skillet, and using your fingers or the back of a spatula, press it out as much as you can into a thin layer.

3 Turn the heat to medium-low and toast the banana-oat mixture for 6 to 8 minutes, or until the underside starts to turn a dark golden brown.

4 Using a spatula, flip the entire layer of granola. It may start to break apart, but it should flip in large pieces. If not, then let it cook for another minute or two.

5 Toast the second side until it turns dark golden brown as well, and the center of the mixture is nearly dry, about another 5 minutes.

6 Let the granola cool for 10 minutes before enjoying. Store in an airtight container for up to 3 days.

FRENCH

Vanilla

OATGU

My Instant Plant Milk (page 199) is the base for this non-fermented plant-based alternative to yogurt. It's extra creamy, with that classic sweet French vanilla taste. If you want more tangy yogurt vibes, add a little more lemon juice than I call for, adding a few drops at a time. Who knew homemade 'gurt could be so easy?

ABOUT 2 CUPS

1 recipe (3¼ cups) Instant Plant Milk (page 199)

3 tablespoons organic confectioners' sugar or maple syrup

1 teaspoon pure vanilla extract

1 teaspoon freshly squeezed lemon juice

Pinch of ground cinnamon (optional)

1 Pour the plant milk into a medium pot over medium-high heat. Whisking often, bring the milk to a gentle simmer. Reduce the heat to medium-low and whisk constantly until the mixture thickens to the texture of a creamy vanilla pudding (or your desired consistency) and reduces to 2½ cups, 10 to 15 minutes. If it doesn't seem to be reducing, you may also want to raise the heat to medium partway through. I like my yogurt creamy, like Siggi's Skyr (they have a great plant-based option).

2 Remove the thickened mixture from the heat and whisk in the sugar, vanilla, lemon juice, and cinnamon (if using) until well combined and smooth. Allow to cool. (It'll thicken a little more as it cools, too.)

3 Transfer the cooled yogurt to a sealed container and place in the fridge for at least 2 hours, preferably overnight. Store in the fridge in a lidded jar or container for up to 3 days.

☆ Try Adding a Flavor!

I like to stir in protein powder or an all-natural flavor like cocoa or chia jam. You can also omit the sweetener, vanilla, and cinnamon for an unflavored yogurt, which is great for savory recipes.

TOAST — TOAST!

My toast to toast! Avocado toast can get a
little old, so try making these variations.

Upside-Down Toast

SERVES 1

1 slice soft sandwich bread

1 teaspoon vegan butter or refined coconut oil

1 teaspoon organic cane sugar

½ teaspoon ground cinnamon

2 to 3 thin slices of fruit, such as apple or peach

Using a cup or rolling pin, flatten the piece of bread and spread it completely with the vegan butter.

On a parchment-lined sheet pan, sprinkle the sugar and cinnamon to make a 4-inch circle directly on the parchment paper. Then lay the fruit slices on top. Press the bread, butter side down, onto the fruit and press the edges to seal the bread to the pan (and around the fruit). Bake at 425°F until golden, about 8 minutes. Flip to serve.

Lemon Bar Toast

SERVES 1

3 tablespoons all-purpose flour

2 tablespoons freshly squeezed lemon juice

1 tablespoon vegan butter or refined coconut oil

1 tablespoon organic cane sugar

Pinch of fine sea salt

2 slices soft sandwich bread

Confectioners' sugar and finely grated lemon zest, for serving

Preheat the oven to 425°F. In a small bowl, stir together the flour, lemon juice, vegan butter, sugar, and salt to form a smooth paste. Spread the mixture evenly on one side of each slice of bread. Place the lemon bread on a sheet pan and bake until the bottom of the bread is dark golden, about 8 minutes. To serve, sprinkle with powdered sugar and lemon zest and cut into thin bar-like strips.

Cheesecake Toast

SERVES 1

1 teaspoon tapioca starch

1 teaspoon water

2 tablespoons vegan cream cheese, softened

1 tablespoon organic cane sugar

1 slice soft sandwich bread

1 tablespoon Mixed Berry Chia Jam (page 223) or store-bought jam

Preheat the oven to 425°F. In a small bowl, stir together the tapioca starch and water. Then add the cream cheese and sugar and stir to combine. Using your fingers, press a 4-inch circle into the center of the bread (you can also use the bottom of a glass). Fill the circle depression with the cream cheese mixture. Place on a sheet pan and bake until the bottom of the toast is dark golden, about 8 minutes. To serve, dollop with the Mixed Berry Chia Jam.

Brown Sugar 'Nana Toast

SERVES 1

1 teaspoon vegan butter or refined coconut oil

1 tablespoon organic light brown sugar

1 teaspoon ground cinnamon, plus more for serving

1 ripe banana, peeled and thinly sliced (use your peel for Banana Peel Bacon, page 76)

1 slice toast, any kind you like

Trail Mix Butter (page 210) or your favorite nut butter, for serving

Pinch of fine sea salt

In a small skillet over medium heat, warm the vegan butter until it starts to melt. Then stir in the sugar and cinnamon. Add the banana and toss to coat. Cook until the sugar melts and begins to caramelize the banana. Top the toasted bread with a thin layer of Trail Mix Butter and the cooked banana. Sprinkle with a pinch of salt and cinnamon before eating.

Banana

Peel

BA

I vow never to throw away old bananas. Sometimes the overripe, extra-sweet ones make a recipe even tastier, and even the peels can have purpose!

Serves
1 TO 2

2 banana peels from very ripe bananas (they should have some browning on them)

2 tablespoons soy sauce

1 tablespoon refined coconut oil

1 tablespoon maple syrup

¼ teaspoon paprika

¼ teaspoon fine sea salt

¼ teaspoon freshly ground black pepper

¼ teaspoon liquid smoke

1 Using the back of a spoon, remove the inner white part of the banana peels. Then rinse and dry the peels under warm water to remove anything you wouldn't want to be eating. In a medium bowl, combine the soy sauce, coconut oil, maple syrup, paprika, salt, pepper, and liquid smoke. Add the banana peels and let marinate for 20 minutes.

2 In a large skillet over medium heat, cook the marinated banana peels until they crisp up some, about 3 minutes per side (they'll crisp up more as they cool).

3 Serve with a side of vegan eggs (see Scramble Me, Please, page 61) or on a BBLT (banana, bacon, lettuce, tomato) sandwich.

French Toast

I love French toast because it melts in your mouth, and it's **SYRUPY** and *sweet*. I love French fries because they're convenient and crispy, and truly, finger foods are *fantastic*. I think most dishes need a crunch element to feel entirely complete, so these **oat-coated** sticks are a little heartier than plain soaked bread, and they hold their shape when you pick one up to dip (even enough to make a Jenga tower), essentially perfecting a **CLASSIC** French toast and reimagining a fry. They're so *good* I wrote a poem about them:

Finger food before noon.
No need for a spoon.
Dip these in syrup and sing a silly little tune
Called "Finger Food Before Noon."

FRIES

Makes

8 TOAST STICKS

¼ cup DIY Oat Flour (page 215) or
store-bought oat flour

2 tablespoons organic cane sugar

1 teaspoon ground cinnamon

1 prepared Flax Egg (page 198)

¼ cup Instant Plant Milk (page 199)
or unsweetened oat milk

2 slices soft sandwich bread

1 to 2 tablespoons vegan butter or
refined coconut oil

Cheap & Sweet Syrup (page 194)
or maple syrup

1 On a plate, using a fork, whisk together the DIY Oat Flour, sugar, and cinnamon. Then in a shallow bowl, whisk together the prepared Flax Egg and plant milk until combined.

2 Stack the bread slices and cut into four equal sections to get 8 sticks by cutting the bread in half vertically, then in half again vertically.

3 Quickly dip a stick into the milk mixture. Then coat it in the oat flour mixture. Do not let the bread soak. Place the dipped stick on a plate or sheet pan. Repeat with the remaining sticks.

4 In a nonstick skillet over medium heat, warm 1 tablespoon of the vegan butter until melted. Add the coated sticks and cook until crispy and golden, 3 to 5 minutes per side. Lower the heat if needed to ensure the inside of the bread is cooked through, but the outside does not burn. Repeat if necessary, adding another tablespoon vegan butter if needed, until all the sticks are cooked.

5 Serve with a side of Cheap & Sweet Syrup for dipping.

BUBBLE BAGEL Bites

Three words: vital wheat gluten. Although this ingredient isn't featured anywhere else in the book, buying a bag of this stuff is worth it solely for this recipe (see What to Do with Vital Wheat Gluten below for other uses). Vital wheat gluten is a protein-packed flour that's commonly used in vegan meat substitutes; it's made from wheat flour that has been processed to remove everything but the gluten. In this recipe, it works to make a practically instant dough that, when cooked at a high temperature, creates a chewy, airy snack that can be ripped apart and stuffed with vegan cream cheese or devoured unstuffed straight from the oven!

Makes
6 BITES

¼ cup vital wheat gluten

¼ cup water

1 tablespoon tapioca starch

¾ teaspoon baking powder

¾ teaspoon white vinegar

¼ teaspoon fine sea salt

1 to 2 tablespoons everything bagel seasoning

Tofu Cream Cheese (page 205) or store-bought vegan cream cheese such as Kite Hill, for serving

1 Preheat the oven to 350°F.

2 In a medium bowl, stir together the vital wheat gluten, water, tapioca starch, baking powder, vinegar, and salt until a shaggy dough forms. The dough will be very wet. Using your hands, knead the dough for 1 to 2 minutes until it becomes smooth.

3 Break the dough into tablespoon-size pieces and roll them into balls roughly 1 inch in diameter.

4 Pour the everything bagel seasoning into a small bowl and roll the balls in it until covered. Place the bites an inch or two apart on an ungreased sheet pan.

5 Bake for 10 minutes, then turn each bite over so it can brown a little more on the other side. Continue baking until they are puffed and golden, 13 to 15 minutes total. Serve with Tofu Cream Cheese. They are best enjoyed right from the oven.

☆ What to Do with Vital Wheat Gluten

Use this protein-rich flour to make homemade seitan, or add a tablespoon to your pizza crust for a chewier bite. I add a teaspoon to my Cinnamon Roll for One (page 88) for a fluffier rise. The general ratio to go by is 1 tablespoon of vital wheat gluten to 2 cups of flour.

Pepper Salmon

Believe it or not, bell peppers are so versatile they can be made to mimic fish! Thin slices of Pepper Salmon serve well as a substitute for lox, or use Pepper Salmon to make smoky salmon cream cheese rolls (see Roll Me Up! below). During roasting, the pepper absorbs tons of flavor from the marinade, so letting it sit overnight is not a bad thing. You may be surprised by how tasty this not-usually-thought-of-to-be-a-fish-substitute vegetable becomes.

 Makes

THE EQUIVALENT TO A 4-OUNCE PACKAGE SMOKED SALMON

1 red bell pepper

1 tablespoon soy sauce

1 tablespoon sesame oil

1 tablespoon seaweed flakes or furikake

1 teaspoon rice vinegar

1 teaspoon organic cane sugar

1 Preheat the oven to 425°F.

2 Put the bell pepper on a sheet pan and roast, turning it every 7 minutes or so to blacken each side, until fully charred, 20 to 25 minutes total. Alternatively, you can also roast the pepper over the flame of a gas stovetop, using tongs to rotate it, until the pepper is completely blackened.

3 Once the pepper has cooled, slice it down one side, from the stem to the bottom, and open it up flat. The idea is to keep the pepper in one long piece. Remove the skin, stem, and seeds; this is easiest done under running water. In a small bowl with a lid (or a resealable bag), stir together the soy sauce, sesame oil, seaweed flakes, rice vinegar, and sugar. Add the roasted, cleaned red pepper and turn it in the marinade to coat. Marinate for a minimum of 20 minutes or up to 24 hours. Once it is marinated, thinly slice and use as desired.

 ## Roll Me Up!

Lay the marinated red pepper flat and spread it with a few tablespoons of vegan cream cheese. Roll it up and cut it into slices about ½ inch thick. Refrigerate until ready to serve.

JAMMY

A childhood favorite, made smaller, customizable, and freshly baked. After making many versions of these, I wonder why savory Pop-Tarts aren't sold in grocery stores? The public is missing out on a conveniently packaged, bite-size stuffed snack, so we will make them for ourselves and pity their loss. Instead of using jam, try stuffing one of these with Kale Pesto Crumble (page 224) and a little plant-based cheese or All-Purpose Cheese (page 203) and leaving off the glaze to see what I mean. Killer.

Makes
4 POP-TARTS

1 cup all-purpose flour

1 tablespoon organic cane sugar

Pinch of fine sea salt

¼ cup vegan butter, cut into ¼-inch cubes, softened

3 to 4 tablespoons cold water

¼ cup Mixed Berry Chia Jam (page 223) or store-bought jam

For the glaze

2 tablespoons organic confectioners' sugar

Few drops of water or lemon juice

1 Preheat the oven to 350°F. Line a sheet pan with parchment paper. Set aside.

2 In a medium bowl, using a fork, whisk together the flour, cane sugar, and salt. Sprinkle in the butter and water. Continue to stir until a dough forms. Divide the dough in half and shape each piece into a rectangle. Wrap each piece in plastic wrap and refrigerate for at least 20 minutes.

3 On a lightly floured surface, roll each piece into a 6 × 8-inch rectangle. The dough should be about ⅛ inch thick.

4 Cut each dough rectangle into 4 even rectangles. You will get 8 (3 × 4-inch) rectangles total.

5 Dollop 1 tablespoon Mixed Berry Chia Jam onto the center of half of the rectangles. Top with the remaining dough squares, and using a fork, crimp together the edges on all sides.

6 Bake until the dough turns golden, 40 to 45 minutes.

7 *Meanwhile, make the glaze:* In a small bowl, whisk together the confectioners' sugar and water until smooth and the consistency of heavy cream. Add more sugar or water to reach the desired consistency. Drizzle over the cooled Pop-Tarts. Let the icing harden before serving.

Pop-Tarts

CINNAM

OVERNIGHT DOUGHS are one of the best *hacks* because the next morning you have a sweet treat that is ready to bake, with *no work* to do. The result here, in addition to the scent of cinnamon wafting through the air, is a soft roll with a chewy golden *edge*, thanks to the addition of vital wheat gluten (see What to Do with Vital Wheat Gluten, page 83, for more about this ingredient).

ROLL FOR

Serves
1

For the dough

4 tablespoons all-purpose flour

1 tablespoon vital wheat gluten (optional; can be replaced with 1 tablespoon of flour)

1 tablespoon organic cane sugar

¼ teaspoon rapid rise yeast

Pinch of fine sea salt

1 tablespoon Instant Plant Milk (page 199) or unsweetened oat milk

1 tablespoon vegan butter, softened to room temperature

For the filling

1 tablespoon refined coconut oil or vegan butter, plus more for coating

1 tablespoon organic cane sugar

1 teaspoon ground cinnamon

For the icing

2 tablespoons confectioners' sugar, plus more as needed

1½ teaspoons unsweetened oat milk, freshly squeezed lemon juice, or water

Drop of pure vanilla extract

1 **Make the dough:** In a medium bowl, stir together the flour, vital wheat gluten, sugar, yeast, and salt. Then add the plant milk and butter and stir until a dough starts to form. Using your hands, bring the dough together and knead it for a minute or two to form a smooth ball. Put the dough ball back in the bowl, cover, and set it in a warm place to rest for one hour (you won't see any rise action happening and that's okay).

2 Lightly coat a small ramekin (about 3½ inches in diameter) or oven-safe mug with butter.

3 **Make the filling:** Divide the dough into two even pieces. On a lightly floured surface, use a rolling pin to roll out each piece of dough into two long strips 12 inches long and 1½ to 2 inches wide. Using a butter knife, spread the two strips evenly all over with the coconut oil. Sprinkle evenly with the sugar and cinnamon. Starting with one strip, roll it up to form a coil, then continue rolling the second strip around the roll. Place the roll in the dish, cover with plastic wrap, and put it in the refrigerator to rise overnight.

4 In the morning, preheat the oven to 350°F and remove the plastic wrap from the roll.

5 Bake the roll until the edges turn golden and the top springs back when you press it lightly, 30 to 35 minutes.

6 **While the roll bakes, make the icing:** In a small bowl, stir together the confectioners' sugar, oat milk, and vanilla until smooth. Add more sugar or milk as needed to get your desired consistency. Spread the icing on top of the cooked roll. The roll is best eaten the day it's baked.

CHEESECAKE-STUFFED *Fruit*

This is one of my favorite ways to turn a piece of fruit into a filling breakfast. For a heartier take, I like to substitute granola for the chia seeds here, or even just use plain oats for a rustic approach to this homey breakfast. Top a cooked half with some vegan vanilla ice cream to make this dish dessert, or just because you want to.

Serves 2 TO 4

2 whole pears, apples, or peaches

⅓ cup unsweetened soy-based yogurt, such as Silk

3 tablespoons vegan cream cheese, softened

1 tablespoon chia seeds

1 teaspoon maple syrup

1 teaspoon freshly squeezed lemon juice

Pinch or two of ground granola and cinnamon, for serving

 Preheat the oven to 375°F. Line a sheet pan with parchment paper. Set aside.

 Slice the pears in half and remove the seeds. Then using a tablespoon, scoop out a cavity about 2 inches in diameter. Then cut a very thin slice off the round cheeks of each fruit half so they sit flat.

 In a small bowl, stir together the yogurt, cream cheese, chia seeds, maple syrup, and lemon juice until smooth and the cream cheese is fully incorporated. Spoon the mixture evenly into the fruit halves, about 2 tablespoons per half. It's okay to heap the mixture.

 Place the filled fruit halves on the prepared sheet pan and bake until the fruit is softened and the cream cheese mixture is slightly browned, about 30 minutes. (The time will vary depending on the type and size of the fruit.) Sprinkle with granola and cinnamon to serve.

A great crepe is fluffy and light—I like to think of it as a cross between a pancake and an Indian dosa. Traditionally made with eggs, the batter is poured into a pan, quickly swirled around until it's nice and thin, cooked on both sides, then stuffed with endless filling possibilities. The technique here is the same, but the batter contains no eggs and fewer ingredients and the result tastes just as good. You can easily make these gluten-free by subbing in GF flour.

Makes

6 (8-INCH) CREPES

1 cup all-purpose flour

¾ cup water (or you can sub in aquafaba, page 198)

½ cup unsweetened almond or oat milk

1 tablespoon organic cane sugar

2 to 3 tablespoons vegan butter, for cooking

Fresh fruit and Magic Vegan Whip (page 229), for topping (optional)

1 In a medium bowl, whisk together the flour, water, almond milk, and sugar until smooth. The batter should be thin, like cream. If it's too thick, whisk in a little water to thin it out.

2 In a large nonstick skillet over medium-low heat, melt 1 to 2 teaspoons of the butter. After it's fully melted, use a spatula to spread it around then add 3 to 4 tablespoons of batter to the pan. Twist and turn the pan to coat it evenly with the batter. The crepe should be thin like a piece of paper. (The bigger your pan, the more batter you'll need.)

3 Return the pan to the heat and cook until the edges begin to curl. Flip and cook until the crepe just turns golden on the underside, another 2 to 3 minutes. Repeat by melting a teaspoon or less of butter then add the batter, swirl, cook, flip and repeat until you've used all the batter. Roll or fold the crepes into quarters to plate and top, if using, with fresh fruit and Magic Vegan Whip or any other toppings or fillings you like.

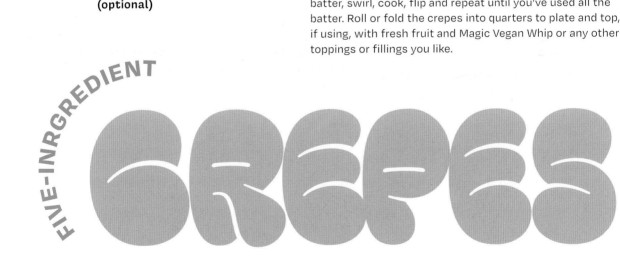
FIVE-INRGEDIENT CREPES

CHEESECAKE-STUFFED FRUIT (PAGE 90)

This spin on waffles is a good savory alternative for breakfast (seems like there are so many more sweet options in this world). I use a Dash Mini Waffle Maker, turning out one thin and crispy tofu treat at a time. You can use a standard waffle maker, too. Either way, if your iron doesn't have a clamp to secure it closed, you'll need to stand and hold the maker tightly closed to get the crispiest texture. Full disclosure: Each waffle can take up to twelve minutes to cook, so here's my trick: I pile up books to press my maker closed. It's effective! I serve these with a caramel-like savory syrup that adds that breakfasty feel. For a full-on sweet morning meal, top with Cheap & Sweet Syrup (page 194) and fruit. Try these crunchy slices as a sub for toast, too.

Makes
4 WAFFLES

1 (14-ounce) block extra-firm tofu

¼ cup tapioca starch or cornstarch

¼ cup Hal's Everything Seasoning (page 187) or your favorite seasoning mix

Cooking spray

Soy Sauce Syrup (page 193), for serving

☆ Try It Sweet!

Skip the seasoning and substitute a mixture of 1 tablespoon sugar and 1 teaspoon ground cinnamon.

1 Remove the tofu block from its package, discarding the liquid, and wrap the tofu with a dishcloth or heavy-duty paper towel (lighter paper towels tend to rip). Place the wrapped block on a rimmed plate or sheet pan and weigh down with a heavy pot or cast-iron skillet for 20 minutes.

2 Once the block is pressed, unwrap it and carefully slice the block horizontally into 4 large pieces, as if you were cutting a cake round in half or a sub roll lengthwise. Each thin rectangular piece should be about ¼ inch thick.

3 Preheat your waffle iron to get it nice and hot.

4 Combine the tapioca starch and Hal's seasoning on a plate and use a fork to mix together well. Gently press a tofu slice into the starch mixture, coating both sides. Repeat with the remaining pieces.

5 Coat your waffle iron with cooking spray and let it heat for 1 more minute. Place as many slices of coated tofu as you can fit comfortably in your waffle iron. Clamp or hold it closed or place a weight on your iron and cook the tofu for about 8 minutes, then check to see if it looks golden and crispy. If not, keep cooking, checking every 2 minutes or so until it is! Repeat with the remaining tofu slices that need to be cooked. Serve with Soy Sauce Syrup.

CRISPY *Tofu* WAFF

WITH SOY SAUCE SYRUP

Banana Baby

PANCA

These bite-size banana-y pillows are delightful. Sometimes I slice strawberries and bananas and add them to the batter after I've blended it to make fruit-filled pancake bites, but they're just as good when the plain cooked pancakes are thrown into a bowl and topped with syrup, yogurt, or fresh fruit. The protein powder makes them extra filling and nutritious in the morning.

Makes
10 TO 12 (2-INCH) PANCAKES

½ cup Instant Plant Milk (page 199) or
unsweetened oat milk

1 ripe banana, peeled

½ cup old-fashioned rolled oats

2 tablespoons of your favorite unflavored or
vanilla vegan protein powder

1 tablespoon chia seeds

½ teaspoon baking powder

½ teaspoon pure vanilla extract

Pinch of ground cinnamon, plus more for serving

1 to 2 tablespoons vegan butter

Cheap & Sweet Syrup (page 194) or
maple syrup, for serving

1 In a blender, combine the plant milk, banana, oats, unflavored protein powder, chia seeds, baking powder, vanilla, and cinnamon. Blend until smooth.

2 Melt 1 teaspoon butter in a skillet over medium-high heat. Pour 1 tablespoon batter onto the skillet, and using the back of the spoon, form a 2-inch round. Repeat, making as many rounds as the skillet will hold. Reduce the heat to medium-low. Cook until bubbles form on the top and the bottoms turn golden. Then flip and cook until cooked through, another 1 to 2 minutes. Both sides should be golden. Add another teaspoon of butter and repeat until you've cooked all the batter. Serve with Cheap & Sweet Syrup and a sprinkle of cinnamon.

FRUITY Oat SQUARES

These are my version of a soft and chewy granola bar, but cut small, into bite-size squares.

You want to sub jam for the cooked berries? I wouldn't be mad about it. You'll need 2 to 3 tablespoons (try my Mixed Berry Chia Jam, page 223). It'll make the process quicker, and the end bite just as delicious.

Makes
8 SQUARES

1 overripe banana, peeled

2 tablespoons vegan butter, softened to room temperature

½ cup old-fashioned rolled oats

1 teaspoon ground cinnamon

1 tablespoon plus 1 teaspoon maple syrup

Pinch of fine sea salt

½ cup frozen mixed berries

1 Preheat the oven to 350°F. Line a sheet pan with parchment paper. Set aside.

2 In a medium bowl, using a fork, mash together the banana and butter until smooth. Sprinkle in the oats, cinnamon, the 1 teaspoon maple syrup, and salt and stir the mixture until thoroughly combined.

3 On the prepared sheet pan, shape the banana mixture into a 5-inch square that's about ¼ inch thick. Bake until the oats darken and the mixture feels firm, 20 to 25 minutes. Meanwhile, in a small saucepan over medium heat, combine the fruit and the 1 tablespoon maple syrup, mashing them together with a fork or masher, and continue cooking until the water cooks off and the mixture is reduced by half to ¼ cup and becomes jam-like, about 5 minutes, lowering the heat if needed to prevent any burning.

4 Let the baked oat bar cool, then slice it in half, spread the cooked fruit onto one side, and top with the other half as you would a sandwich.

5 Cut into 8 equal squares and enjoy. Store in an airtight container at room temperature for up to 2 days.

Quinoa

I wish I had grown up with a boxed version of this Quinoa Crunch in the cereal aisle. It's one of those hidden healthy things that shouldn't work but somehow does, and theoretically could be eaten throughout the week but ends up disappearing in a day. And for those who don't love regular cooked quinoa, I find this crunchy version is more universally accepted. If you are on the fence, I say go ahead, give it a try.

Serves
1

½ cup sweetened or unsweetened oat or almond milk, depending on your preference

1 to 2 tablespoons creamy peanut butter

½ cup Quinoa Crunch for Sweet Treats! (see page 227)

½ banana, peeled, then sliced or diced

Toppings like nuts and seeds (optional)

1 teaspoon Cheap & Sweet Syrup (page 194) or maple syrup (optional)

Pinch of ground cinnamon (optional)

In a cereal bowl, whisk together ¼ cup of the oat milk and 2 teaspoons of the peanut butter until smooth. Continue to whisk slowly and add the remaining ¼ cup milk and 4 teaspoons of peanut butter in stages until smooth. (Looser peanut butters blend better—if your peanut butter does completely emulsify, that's okay—it'll still be delicious.) Add the Quinoa Crunch for Sweet Treats! and the banana and sprinkle with any toppings you'd like (if using). To sweeten up your cereal, drizzle with Cheap & Sweet Syrup and a pinch of cinnamon.

☆ Customizable Cereal Milk?

Hell yeah! Replace the peanut butter and banana with 1 tablespoon raspberry jam and ¼ cup fresh berries, or any flavor jam you like. Or use both for a PB&J breakfast treat!

CRUNCH CEREAL

3. EAS

M

2 CUPS GROUND BEEF CRUMBLES

1 tablespoon extra-virgin olive oil

2 cups cooked brown lentils (see How to Cook Brown Lentils, below)

2 tablespoons Hal's Everything Seasoning (page 187)

Fine sea salt and freshly ground black pepper

Crispy, savory, and an exceptional sub in most all traditional beef-based dishes (think tacos, burgers, Bolognese, or protein on a veggie bowl), Lentil Ground Beef is the answer.

1 In a skillet over medium heat, warm the olive oil for a few minutes, or just until it starts to shimmer. Add the cooked lentils, mashing most of them with the back of a spatula. Then spread them in the skillet to create a thin layer. Leave them alone—don't be tempted to stir! Let them cook for 5 to 7 minutes, then turn a small bit of the lentils with the spatula. You should see them getting slightly golden and crispy. If not, let them cook a bit more. Then flip all the lentils and sprinkle with the Hal's seasoning.

2 Continue to stir and toss until ground-beef-like crumbles form, cooking until the lentil crumbles are browned, about 6 minutes longer. There is a fine line between cooking until golden and cooking until they are overdone. It's better to err on the side of underdone; otherwise the crumbles dry out. Season with salt and pepper if needed. Use as desired. Store in the fridge for up to 3 days.

HOW TO COOK BROWN LENTILS

1 cup dried brown lentils

1 bay leaf

About 2½ cups water, depending on the size of your saucepan

½ teaspoon fine sea salt

Using a strainer, rinse the lentils and remove any stones or foreign matter. Put the lentils in a medium saucepan, add the bay leaf, and cover with 3 to 4 inches of water. Bring the water to a boil. Then lower the heat and simmer, covered, until the lentils are tender but still firm, 20 to 25 minutes. Keep an eye on them to make sure they don't boil dry. Add more water if needed. Drain the lentils and use as desired.

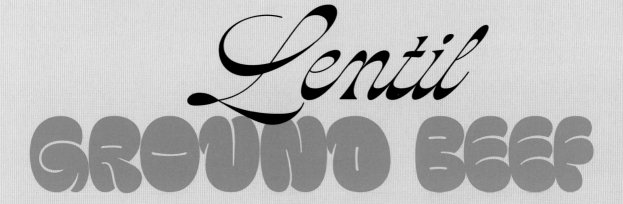

Lentil GROUND BEEF

BOLOGNESE Spaghetti Squash BOWLS

I cooked a lot for my family and myself during the COVID-19 pandemic—it was the first time we were at home together since I was little. I especially sought out gluten-free options for my sister, who has celiac disease and hates manual labor, and this one-dish meal was a big hit. It has all the homey, classic feelings of spaghetti with meat sauce, but is veg forward. You can also toss the spaghetti-like squash noodles with other sauces, such as Kale Pesto Crumble (page 224). This dish reheats very well. I like to scoop out the inside and take it to go for lunch the next day just as I would pasta.

2 BOWLS

1 large spaghetti squash

2 tablespoons extra-virgin olive oil

Fine sea salt and freshly ground black pepper

Lentil Bolognese Sauce (page 107)

½ cup shredded All-Purpose Cheese (page 203) or store-bought vegan mozzarella or Parmesan

1 Preheat the oven to 425°F. Line a sheet pan with parchment paper. Set aside.

2 Using a sharp fork, poke the squash all over. Then slice it in half the short way, to make 2 bowls. You may need to trim the ends flat so the bowls sit evenly. Using a spoon, scoop out the seeds and discard.

3 Rub the insides of the squash halves with the olive oil and sprinkle liberally with salt and pepper. Place the squash halves cavity side down on the sheet pan and roast until they are soft and you can pierce them with a fork, 30 to 35 minutes.

4 Preheat your broiler while you make the spaghetti.

5 When the squash has finished roasting and cool enough to handle, using a fork, scrape the insides of the squash to make spaghetti-like strings. Taste the squash and season with salt and pepper if needed. Then push down the spaghetti to make room for the sauce. Spoon the Bolognese evenly into the two cavities until full. Sprinkle with the All-Purpose Cheese, dividing it evenly between the two bowls as well.

6 Return the squash bowls to the oven and broil until the cheese is bubbly and golden, 3 to 5 minutes. Serve immediately.

Lentil Bolognese Sauce

MAKES ABOUT 2½ CUPS

1½ cups of your favorite red spaghetti sauce

1 batch (2 cups) Lentil Ground Beef (page 104)

¼ cup water

In a medium saucepan over medium heat, combine the sauce, Lentil Ground Beef, and water. Simmer, stirring occasionally, until thickened and slightly reduced, about 10 minutes. Use for Bolognese Spaghetti Squash Bowls (page 105) or store in a lidded jar or airtight container in the fridge for up to 3 days.

KILLER

Chili is a kind of **CATCHALL** dish in my opinion—probably because I've never made a batch that tastes *exactly* the same. Think of chili as a *magic* pot, and throw in whatever ingredients you have on hand, including the occasional **espresso** or olives or **RANDOM** produce item, and let her cook. When it's colder out, I *really* love adding cinnamon. Okay, shutting up now. I'll leave it to you to add what you want to make this chili yours.

CHILI

WITH

Serves
4

2 tablespoons extra-virgin olive oil

1 medium yellow or white onion, chopped (about 1 cup)

1 (15-ounce) can beans (black, pinto, kidney, or garbanzo), drained and rinsed

¼ cup chopped raw walnuts

2 tablespoons minced garlic

2 tablespoons soy sauce

1 tablespoon Cheap & Sweet Syrup (page 194) or maple syrup

1 tablespoon chili powder

1 teaspoon paprika

1 teaspoon ground cinnamon

1 teaspoon ground cumin

½ teaspoon fine sea salt

¼ teaspoon white pepper

¼ teaspoon cayenne pepper

1 batch (2 cups) Lentil Ground Beef (page 104) or 2 cups Gardein Plant-Based Ground Be'f

1 (15-ounce) can diced tomatoes

1½ cups water with 1 bouillon cube dissolved in it, or vegetable broth

Grated Potato Cheese (page 204) or vegan yogurt and minced green onion, for serving

1. In a large heavy-bottom saucepan or Dutch oven over medium heat, warm the olive oil until it just starts to shimmer. Add the onion and cook, stirring occasionally, until translucent, about 10 minutes, reducing the heat to medium-low if the onion is starting to burn.

2. Next add the beans, walnuts, garlic, soy sauce, Cheap & Sweet Syrup, chili powder, paprika, cinnamon, cumin, salt, white pepper, and cayenne pepper. Cook over medium-high heat, stirring, until fragrant, about 5 minutes.

3. Add the Lentil Ground Beef, tomatoes, and water/bouillon mix. Cover, reduce the heat to low and simmer until some of the liquid cooks down about ½ inch, or for 20 to 25 minutes.

4. Serve with a sprinkle of grated cheese and/or a dollop of yogurt and a sprinkle of minced green onion. Store leftovers in the fridge for up to 4 days.

Lentil GROUND BEEF

TOFU-SHELL *Taco* NIGHT

I call this dish a project because you make *both* the tortillas and the filling from scratch, so it's best for a day when you're in the mood to cook. A Tuesday would be ideal. And possibly a margarita while you work. The tofu shell, as I call it, is made from Tofu Dough (page 216), and using it to make traditional tortillas backs how versatile the dough is. This dish also highlights the crispiness and deliciousness of Lentil Ground Beef (page 104), another often-used recipe of mine, as the filling. It's the hero of this meal—a good "old-fashioned, yet not so old-fashioned" plant-packed taco.

Makes 6 TACOS

½ batch Tofu Dough (page 216)

All-purpose flour, for rolling out

4 teaspoons extra-virgin olive oil, or more as needed

1 batch (2 cups) Lentil Ground Beef (page 104)

½ teaspoon ground cumin

½ teaspoon paprika

For serving

1 recipe Spicy Mayo (page 197)

2 romaine lettuce leaves, finely chopped

1 tomato, diced

¼ cup Savory Chickpea Crunches (page 226) (optional)

1 Divide the tofu dough into 6 equal pieces and roll into small balls. Lightly flour your work surface, and one at a time, using a rolling pin or bottle, roll out each piece into a 5-inch round tortilla. Lay them out on a sheet pan. (Don't stack them, as they may stick.)

2 In a medium skillet over medium-high heat, add 1 teaspoon of the olive oil. Then one by one, cook the tortillas until little bubbles appear on the surface, about 1 minute 30 seconds Then flip and cook for another 1 minute 30 seconds, until golden spots appear on the underside; add more of the oil if needed as you cook. Transfer the cooked tortillas to a plate lined with a cloth, cover, and set aside.

3 In the same skillet, heat 2 teaspoons of olive oil over medium heat and toss in the Lentil Ground Beef. Sprinkle with the cumin and paprika. Toss to combine and cook, continuing to gently toss, until the ground beef is just warmed through.

4 Arrange a platter with a bowl of ground beef at the center, a stack of tofu tortillas, a side of Spicy Mayo, chopped lettuce, diced tomato, and Savory Chickpea Crunches, if using.

Use Up Your Dough!

- Make additional tortillas and freeze them.
- Make a half batch of Tofu Pops (page 22).
- Use it as a substitute for the spinach crust in the Personal Pizza (page 136).

Lasagna ROLL-UPS

For this recipe, noodles are rolled individually to create hearty pockets of flavor. They have all the elements of a classic lasagna (plus a satisfying crunch), and they bake in almost a quarter of the time. Also, because there's no resting time, either, they can be eaten right away. And when you cut into them, the swirl is a pretty surprise. They're easy to store, too, so double this recipe and keep some roll-ups in your freezer for an easy meal later on.

Makes
6 TO 8 ROLL-UPS

1 batch (2 cups) Lentil Ground Beef (page 104) or 2 cups store-bought plant protein of choice

2 cups firmly packed bagged spinach leaves, finely chopped

⅓ cup Homemade Vegan Mayo (page 196) or store-bought vegan mayo

1 cup unsweetened almond or oat milk

⅔ cup all-purpose flour

½ cup Hal's Everything Seasoning (page 187) or vegan seasoned bread crumbs

½ cup panko bread crumbs

8 lasagna noodles, cooked, run under cold water, and patted dry

Cooking spray

1 cup Kale Pesto Crumble made with 1 cup extra-virgin olive oil (page 224) or 2 cups of your favorite jarred marinara sauce, warmed

 Preheat the oven to 400°F. Line a sheet pan with parchment paper. Set aside.

 In a medium bowl, stir together the cooled Lentil Ground Beef, spinach, and mayo until smooth.

 In a shallow bowl, whisk together the unsweetened almond milk and flour. On a plate, combine the Hal's seasoning and panko. Lay out a noodle flat and spread the surface with 2 to 3 tablespoons of the lentil mixture. Roll up the noodle and dip the entire roll in the milk-flour mixture to coat it. Then put it on the plate with the seasoning and spoon the mixture over it to coat the roll. (If you roll it in the seasoning, it'll start to get clumpy.) Transfer the roll to the prepared sheet pan and repeat with the remaining noodles and filling.

 Lightly coat the rolls with cooking spray. Bake until the crust is golden, 15 to 20 minutes. Top each roll with 2 tablespoons of Kale Pesto Crumble or ¼ cup marinara sauce, or both! Enjoy.

WATERMELON

Cooking a watermelon may seem **STRANGE**. When you marinate watermelon flesh, though, it pulls out some of its moisture. Then when it's baked, something *magical* happens, and you get a soft and creamy, **wonderfully** satisfying tuna substitute. I like to use it in this **POKE-LIKE** bowl, which is really like an open-faced **sushi roll.** Add *whatever* you like here: radishes, carrots, spinach, or anything you fancy.

Tuna Bowl

2 BOWLS

2 tablespoons soy sauce

2 tablespoon furikake or crushed seaweed, plus more for serving

1 teaspoon minced garlic

1 teaspoon sesame seeds, plus more for serving

¼ teaspoon ground black pepper

¼ teaspoon red pepper flakes

¼ teaspoon sesame oil

2 cups (1-inch cubes) seedless watermelon

2 cups One Week's Worth of Sushi Rice (page 186)

1 cup finely chopped iceberg lettuce

¼ cup diced cucumber

¼ cup diced mango

½ avocado, sliced

Spicy Mayo (page 197), for serving

Sliced green onion and/or fresh cilantro (optional)

 In a medium bowl, stir together the soy sauce, furikake, garlic, sesame seeds, black pepper, pepper flakes, and sesame oil. Add the watermelon cubes and marinate in the fridge for 2 hours.

 Preheat the oven to 400°F.

3 Put the cubes on a parchment-lined sheet pan and roast until the cubes are somewhat firm when pressed, 15 to 20 minutes.

 Turn off the oven and let the watermelon cubes continue to dehydrate in the oven, with the door closed, for another hour.

5 Divide the sushi rice between two shallow serving bowls and top with even-size piles of lettuce, cucumber, mango, avocado, and watermelon tuna in each bowl. Drizzle with Spicy Mayo and a sprinkle of furikake, sesame seeds, and green onion and/or cilantro (if using).

☆ Freeze It!

I like to use baby sugar watermelons to make tuna, and I usually end up using only half the melon. Use the other half for Two-Ingredient (No Bananas!) Ice Cream (page 170), subbing frozen watermelon for the berries.

CRISPY RICE

These are essentially a meal in a ball. Hearty and satisfying, they are a great way to use up leftover rice. You can also use One Week's Worth of Sushi Rice (page 186) if you are craving these and don't have leftovers. The most important thing is to reheat the rice before starting. You don't want it too warm, but you also want it warm enough to be sticky and malleable. I also like to wrap these rice balls in toasted nori for an onigiri feel.

Makes

4 TO 5 RICE BALLS

1⅔ cups One Week's Worth of Sushi Rice (page 186) or leftover cooked rice

1 tablespoon white or rice vinegar (optional)

¼ cup shredded cucumber

¼ cup shredded carrot

¼ cup drained and crumbled firm tofu

1 tablespoon vegan cream cheese

1 tablespoon soy sauce, plus more for serving

2 tablespoons sesame seeds

2 tablespoons sesame oil, plus more as needed, for frying

1 First, warm the rice. Put it in a microwave-safe medium bowl, sprinkle it lightly with water, and heat it in the microwave for a minute or two. Don't have a microwave? Put the rice in a skillet, add one to two tablespoons of water, and warm it on the stovetop.

2 If using prepared sushi rice, skip the following step. If using unseasoned leftover cooked rice, drizzle it with the white vinegar. Stir to combine.

3 Squeeze the shredded cucumber to release any water, then put it in another medium bowl and add the carrot, tofu, cream cheese, and soy sauce. Stir until well combined.

4 On a piece of plastic wrap about 12 inches long, sprinkle a thin layer of sesame seeds and put about ⅓ cup of the rice on top, flattening it with wet hands to form a 4- to 5-inch circle. Dollop 1 tablespoon of the veggie-cream cheese mixture onto the center of the flattened rice (leave the edges of the rice uncovered by the filling). Then grab all four ends of the plastic wrap and join them at the center, twisting and squeezing to form a ball. Undo the plastic wrap and repeat with the remaining rice and filling.

5 In a nonstick skillet over medium heat, warm the sesame oil. Fry the rice balls for 2 to 3 minutes per side, cooking until the entire ball is golden and crispy. Continue until all the balls are cooked, adding more oil to the pan as needed. Serve with soy sauce for dipping.

FLAKY FISH 'N'

Canned artichokes are for so much more than just a creamy dip. I like the layered texture of the leaves, which in my opinion mimics flaky fish, so they are perfect for this recipe. I opt for using sliced fingerling potatoes for the chips, as they are an easy way to get that flattened French fry feel that British chips seem to have.

Serves
2

For the Salt Vinegar Chips

1 cup warm water

½ cup white vinegar

1 tablespoon fine sea salt, plus more for seasoning

1 pound fingerling potatoes

For the Artichoke Fish

½ cup all-purpose flour

⅓ cup tapioca starch or cornstarch

1 teaspoon baking powder

½ teaspoon fine sea salt, plus more for seasoning

½ teaspoon paprika

½ teaspoon dried dill

1 Evenly space two racks in your oven to the second and fourth slots, or the equivalent, so you can accommodate two sheet pans at once. Preheat the oven to 400°F. Line two sheet pans with parchment paper. Set aside.

2 **First, prepare the chips:** Combine the warm water, vinegar, and salt in a large bowl and set aside. Next, cut the potatoes vertically to get 4 to 5 "chips" per potato. Put the potatoes in the vinegar water as you cut them. Soak the potatoes for 20 to 30 minutes. Then rinse and dry completely.

3 **Make the fish:** In a medium bowl, whisk together the flour, tapioca starch, baking powder, salt, paprika, dill, pickle juice, and 1 tablespoon of the olive oil. Then add the water and whisk again until smooth. Using a fork, dip the artichoke pieces into the batter until fully coated, allowing the excess to drip off, and transfer to one of the prepared sheet pans, leaving an inch or so between each piece. Bake until the coating is on the darker side of golden brown, 20 to 25 minutes.

CHIPS

½ cup pickle juice, or a bit less than ½ cup water and 3 tablespoons white vinegar

2 tablespoons extra-virgin olive oil

½ cup water

1 (15-ounce) can quartered artichoke hearts, drained and patted dry

Fish 'n' Chips Sauce (recipe here)

4   Meanwhile, transfer the soaked and dried potatoes to the second sheet pan. Sprinkle with the remaining tablespoon oil and a few pinches of salt and toss to coat and bake. Flip the potatoes after about 10 minutes of baking and continue to cook until they are golden brown on both sides, another 10 minutes or so. Both the fish and chips should be done within 25 minutes total cooking time.

Fish 'n' Chips Sauce

MAKES ABOUT ½ CUP

¼ cup unsweetened soy-based yogurt, such as Silk

¼ cup minced pickle

1 teaspoon dried dill

1 to 2 tablespoons freshly squeezed lemon juice

1 teaspoon maple syrup

In a small bowl, stir together the yogurt, pickle, dill, lemon juice, and maple syrup until thoroughly combined. Serve with Flaky Fish 'n' Chips.

Mushroom
PULLED PORK

With a nice meaty texture, this mushroom blend makes such a good sandwich and is conveniently gluten-free (that is, when you make Hal's Everything Seasoning gluten-free). I don't even add slaw as you would with pulled pork—I like to let the 'shrooms shine. And it's easy to make. You can use any brand of vegan barbecue sauce (I like Primal Kitchen) or for an Asian spin, substitute teriyaki sauce for barbecue. You can easily make this ahead, too, as the flavors get even better as they mingle in the fridge.

Makes
2 PILED-HIGH SANDWICHES

12 ounces mushrooms, such as king oyster, portobello, shiitake, enoki, or any combination

3 tablespoons extra-virgin olive oil

3 tablespoons of your favorite barbecue sauce

3 tablespoons Hal's Everything Seasoning (page 187)

1 tablespoon tapioca starch or cornstarch

2 sandwich buns or gluten-free buns, for serving

1 Preheat the oven to 400°F. Line a sheet pan with parchment paper. Set aside.

2 Shred the mushrooms with a fork or grater (use the largest holes on a box grater). You should get about 4 cups. Put the shredded 'shrooms into a large bowl and add the olive oil, barbecue sauce, Hal's seasoning, and tapioca starch. Toss until all the 'shrooms are thoroughly coated.

3 Spread in a single layer on the prepared sheet pan and roast until the mushrooms start to crisp ever so slightly on the edges and become softened, about 25 minutes. Divide the barbecue mushrooms between two buns and serve. You can also store the mushroom in the fridge for up to 3 days and reheat before serving on buns.

Air-Fryer

SMOKY

TOFU

TIPS

I wrote this recipe especially for my best friend, the air fryer, because she cooks it better than anyone. Similar to the unexpected method of baking watermelon for a fish substitute (see page 115), the process used to transform tofu to a meaty substitute may be surprising, too: freezing!

Because tofu is mostly water, freezing helps remove the moisture content, changing the texture to a chewier, denser bite. It also creates pockets that helps frozen, then defrosted tofu absorb marinades better. If you compare never frozen and frozen tofu side by side, I guarantee you'll taste a difference. If you have someone in your life who doubts tofu, I would make this recipe for them. Add a little sriracha if you want to spice things up.

Serves
2 TO 4

1 (14-ounce) block firm tofu, frozen and then thawed in the package

6 tablespoons soy sauce

3 tablespoons maple syrup

3 tablespoons white vinegar

½ teaspoon fine sea salt

¼ teaspoon freshly ground black pepper

½ cup tapioca starch or cornstarch

Cooking spray

¼ cup hickory-smoked barbecue sauce

1 Remove the defrosted tofu from the package, drain, squeezing out as much water as possible without breaking the tofu block, and pat dry. Cut the tofu block to get 12 bite-size cubes.

2 In a medium shallow bowl or baking dish, whisk together 4 tablespoons of the soy sauce, 2 tablespoons of the maple syrup, 2 tablespoons of the vinegar, and the salt and pepper. Add the tofu cubes and gently turn to coat on all sides with the marinade. Let the tofu marinate for 30 minutes, turning the cubes every 10 minutes or so for even absorption.

3 Preheat the air fryer to 400°F.

4 Meanwhile, pour the tapioca starch onto a plate. When the tofu is done marinating, dip each side of each cube in the starch and lightly coat with cooking spray. Put the coated tips in the tray of an air fryer. Air-fry until crispy and golden, 15 to 20 minutes.

5 While the tips are cooking, in a small bowl, stir together the barbecue sauce and remaining 2 tablespoons of soy sauce, 1 tablespoon of maple syrup, and 1 tablespoon of vinegar. Using a brush, coat the crispy tips with the glaze and cook for another 3 to 5 minutes. Serve immediately.

EASY HOMEMADE PASTAS

Sweet Potato Gnocchi with Lentil Bolognese Sauce

SERVES 2

Gnocchi, the memory foam pillow of the pasta world. You might just be surprised at how easy it is to make this homemade eggless pasta.

1 batch Sweet Potato Dough (page 216)

½ batch Lentil Bolognese Sauce (page 107), heated

Divide the dough into quarters and gently roll each piece into a rope 8 to 10 inches long and ¾ inch in diameter. Using a bench scraper or butter knife, cut each rope into 1-inch gnocchi-like pieces (they'll look like little pillows). Set aside on a plate or sheet pan.

To cook the gnocchi, bring a large pot of salted water to a boil. Using a slotted spoon, gently lower the gnocchi into the boiling water, and stir so it doesn't stick to the bottom of the pot. When the gnocchi float to the top, after about 3 minutes, cook for another 2 to 3 minutes, or until they are cooked through. Remove the cooked gnocchi with a slotted spoon and transfer to a serving dish. Toss with the heated Bolognese sauce and serve.

Snipped Tofu Pasta with Pesto Sauce

SERVES 2

Handmade and hand-snipped, these scrappy pasta noodles—made with a two-ingredient tofu dough and a pasta-shaping method that doesn't require a machine—makes for one of the easiest homemade pastas to prepare.

1 batch Tofu Dough (page 216)

⅓ cup Kale Pesto Crumble (page 224) or jarred pesto sauce

Fresh basil leaves, for garnish (optional)

Divide the dough in half and press each half into a flat round. Bring a large pot of salted water to a boil, and using kitchen shears, snip irregular 1½- to 2-inch pieces of the dough into the boiling water. When the pasta pieces float to the top, after about 3 minutes, cook for another 2 to 3 minutes, or until they are cooked through. Remove the cooked pasta with a slotted spoon and transfer to a serving dish. Top with the Kale Pesto Crumble and fresh basil leaves (if using) and serve.

NOT.

I like to **FULLY** load flat, crispy flour *tortillas* almost like I would a piece of **toast**. I think of this as my version of a tostada, which I know is usually made with corn tortillas, but I like the slightly chewy bite of this **SWEET** sriracha-glazed version. You can also cut the coated tortillas *before* baking to make chips, and dip your way to **deliciousness**.

AVOCA

Makes
4 TOSTADAS

For the Pickle Guac

2 ripe avocados, halved and pitted

1 small cucumber, finely diced

2 tablespoons white vinegar

2 tablespoons finely chopped fresh dill

1 teaspoon dried parsley

½ teaspoon fine sea salt

½ teaspoon freshly ground black pepper

¼ teaspoon mustard powder

¼ teaspoon red pepper flakes

For the tostadas

2 tablespoons sriracha

1 tablespoon maple syrup or sweetener of choice

1 tablespoon extra-virgin olive oil

4 (4- to 6-inch) soft flour tortillas

Diced raw onion and flaky salt, for serving

Rice Paper Bacon Snack Strips (page 28), for topping (optional)

1 Preheat the oven to 350°F. Line 2 sheet pans with parchment paper. Set aside.

2 **Make the Pickle Guac:** Scoop out the avocados into a medium bowl and mash very lightly with a fork. Add the cucumber, vinegar, dill, parsley, salt, black pepper, mustard powder, and pepper flakes and mash a little more until the ingredients are evenly combined while still maintaining some chunks.

3 **Make the tostadas:** Next, in a small bowl, stir together the sriracha, maple syrup, and olive oil. Using a basting brush, coat both sides of each tortilla with the spicy maple sauce and lay in a single layer on the prepared sheet pans. Bake until toasted and the tortillas turn golden on the edges, 3 to 5 minutes per side (the tortillas will crisp up more as they cool).

4 Once the tortillas are cooled and crisp, top with 3 to 4 tablespoons of Pickle Guac, sprinkle with onion and flaky salt, and top with Rice Paper Bacon Snack Strips, if using, and serve.

00-Toast

THICK AND CHEWY
EGGPLANT

I will **NEVER** get sick of noodles in any form. I especially like this *eggplant* version as a replacement for takeout lo mein. They come together **fast** (no need to boil!) and they are *all* vegetable—no wheat belly here. To make them even more jam-packed with **VEG**, toss in spinach, edamame, cabbage, or *anything* you have at the same time you cook the onion and pepper.

NOOODLES

Serves
2

- 1 large eggplant, peeled and ends trimmed
- 4 tablespoons soy sauce
- 2 tablespoons organic light brown sugar
- 2 teaspoons minced garlic
- 4 teaspoons sesame seeds
- Fine sea salt and freshly ground black pepper
- 3 tablespoons sesame oil
- ½ large red onion, sliced (about 1 cup)
- 1 red bell pepper, cleaned and sliced
- Green onion sliced on the bias, for garnish (optional)

1 Slice the peeled eggplant in half lengthwise, then cut each half into ½-inch slices that are the full length of the eggplant (not rounds). Then stack the slices and cut them longways to create long noodle-like strips.

2 Next, in a medium bowl, combine the soy sauce, brown sugar, garlic, 2 teaspoons of the sesame seeds, and salt and pepper to taste.

3 In a medium skillet over medium heat, warm 1 tablespoon of the oil until it shimmers. Add the onion and bell pepper and cook, stirring, until softened, 5 to 8 minutes.

4 Add the remaining 2 tablespoons oil and heat for a few seconds. Then add the eggplant noodles and cook, stirring occasionally, until soft, about 5 minutes. Reduce the heat to low and pour the soy sauce mixture over the cooked vegetables. Toss to coat. Cook, stirring quickly, until the sugar in the sauce dissolves, about 5 minutes.

5 Remove from the heat and divide between two bowls. Sprinkle with the remaining 2 teaspoons sesame seeds, garnish with green onion (if using) and serve.

Chopped

Serves
1

8 to 10 lettuce leaves, such as romaine or butter

2 slices vegan white cheese, such as Chao Creamy Original

1 piece of toast

1 small cucumber, quartered lengthwise

3 to 4 tomato slices

Other salad toppings of your choice (get creative!)

2 to 3 tablespoons Ranchy Dressing (page 192)

Few pinches of fine sea salt and freshly ground black pepper

Handful of roasted almonds

I once went to a salad place where they chopped your salad by cutting it with scissors. Then I realized this is a thing. You can actually buy scissors that fit the shape of a bowl and chop your own. There's just something about a finely chopped salad that goes down really well, and the distribution of ingredients is incredible.

Starting with a base of lettuce leaves, stack the salad ingredients one on top of the other: cheese, toast, cucumber, tomato, and any other toppings you'd like to include. Drizzle the dressing over the stack, season with a few pinches of salt and pepper, and using kitchen shears or a chef's knife, begin to chop the ingredients, tossing as you go. Once the salad is finely chopped and well dressed, transfer it to a serving bowl, sprinkle with almonds and more salt and pepper if needed, and enjoy.

Personal PIZZA (IT'S GREEN!)

Frozen pizza can be great, but the number of good options slims down once you start searching for vegan versions, so I decided to create my own. When I want pizza that's plant-based, I don't mind it also being loaded with plants, so I went for it—I blend spinach into the crust of this vegan pizza (it's such a great way to finish off a bag of greens!) and top the cheese with a heap of veggies like 'shrooms, peppers, and olives. You could replace the spinach in the dough with de-stemmed kale or even steamed carrot for an orange 'za. And get creative with the toppings, too. Make this pizza a personal one!

Makes
1 (7-INCH) PIZZA

2 tablespoons extra-virgin olive oil, plus more for coating

1 cup firmly packed bagged spinach

2 tablespoons water

⅔ cup all-purpose flour, plus more for rolling out the dough

½ teaspoon baking powder

¼ teaspoon fine sea salt

¼ cup jarred marinara sauce

¼ cup grated All-Purpose Cheese (page 203) or store-bought grated vegan mozzarella

Pizza toppings, such as 5 to 6 raw mushrooms, sliced bell peppers, sliced black olives, or your favorites

1. Preheat the oven to 425°F. Lightly coat a sheet pan with olive oil. Set aside.

2. Add the spinach, olive oil, and water to a blender and process until liquified and smooth. In a medium bowl, stir together the flour, baking powder, and salt. Pour in the spinach mixture and stir until a shaggy dough forms. Using your hands, bring the dough together into a ball.

3. Sprinkle your work surface lightly with a tablespoon or two of flour and knead the dough ball for a few minutes until it's smooth but not wet. If it's sticky, add another 1 to 2 tablespoons flour and continue to knead the dough until it bounces back when you poke it gently with your finger.

4. With a rolling pin, roll out the dough into a 7-inch round that's about ⅛ inch thick (the crust rises a little in the oven).

5. Transfer the dough round to the prepared sheet pan and top with the marinara sauce, All-Purpose Cheese, and any veggie toppings you are using.

6. Bake until the cheese has melted and the edges and underside of the crust turn golden, 18 to 20 minutes. Cut into slices and serve.

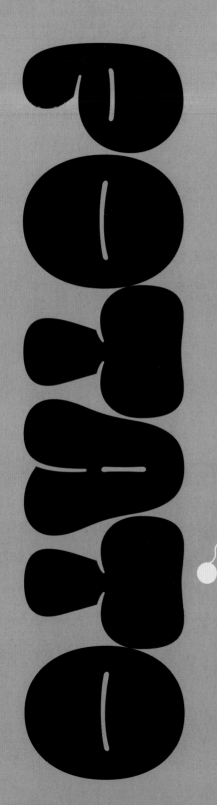

Potatoes are **GREAT** in every form, so why not multiple forms in one recipe? These *nachos* are crispy with **stretchy**, gooey potato cheese and a combination of toppings that makes for a satisfying bite with each chip pick. It's a **BEAUTIFUL** dish because it's *messy*, so don't be afraid to pile ingredients on **top** of your base and see where things go. For a more even distribution, lay your chips flat on a plate or **TRAY** and sprinkle the ingredients evenly on top. However you nacho, you go!

1 batch Sweet Potato Chips
(page 34)

1 batch Potato Cheese, grated
(page 204)

To make your nachos, place a layer of Sweet Potato Chips on a microwave- or oven-safe platter, add a layer with some of your favorite toppings, and sprinkle with grated Potato Cheese. Microwave until the cheese has melted, about 45 seconds, or heat in a 350°F oven for about 8 minutes.

TOPPING IDEAS

Lentil Ground Beef (page 104)

Shredded lettuce

Savory Chickpea Crunches (page 226)

Avocado

Pickles

Fresh cilantro

Shredded lettuce

Diced tomatoes

Pickle Guac (page 129)

Olives

Canned corn, drained

Jalapeños

Fresh lime wedges

chos

ARTICHOKE DIP

This **VEGGIE** burger is a thing of its own, embracing its **authentic** self without a black bean or soy protein in sight. It's creamy, *rich*, and so flavorful that you really don't need any condiments, but of course I can't **RESIST** a little of Hal's Everything Sauce—because I put it on *everything!* When choosing your 'shrooms, look for *portobello* caps that are the size of a burger bun. Want to make this **gluten-free?** Use gluten-free panko and your favorite grain-free **BUN**!

'Shroom Burgers

Makes
4 BURGERS

4 medium portobello mushrooms that are on the thinner side, de-stemmed

4 tablespoons extra-virgin olive oil

¼ teaspoon fine sea salt, plus more for seasoning

Freshly ground black pepper

1 (15-ounce) can chopped artichokes, strained and patted dry

½ cup firmly packed bagged spinach, finely chopped

⅓ cup Homemade Vegan Mayo (page 196) or store-bought vegan mayo

⅓ cup unsweetened soy-based yogurt, such as Silk

¾ cup shredded All-Purpose Cheese (page 203) or store-bought

6 tablespoons panko bread crumbs

1 tablespoon freshly squeezed lemon juice

1 teaspoon minced garlic

½ teaspoon onion powder

½ teaspoon dried parsley

¼ teaspoon red pepper flakes

4 burger buns, Hal's Everything Sauce (page 189), lettuce, and tomato, for serving

1 Line a sheet pan with parchment paper. Set aside.

2 Using the edge of a spoon, scrape the mushroom gills from the underside of the caps until they're mostly hollow, and discard the gills. Rub the mushroom caps all over using 2 tablespoons of the olive oil, and season with a few pinches of the salt and pepper.

3 In a medium bowl, combine the artichokes, spinach, mayo, yogurt, ½ cup of the cheese, 4 tablespoons of the panko, the lemon juice, garlic, onion powder, parsley, pepper flakes, the remaining ¼ teaspoon salt, and a few pinches of black pepper. Place the 'shrooms hollowed side up on the prepared sheet pan and fill them with the spinach-artichoke mixture, dividing it evenly among the 4 caps. Sprinkle the remaining ¼ cup cheese and 2 tablespoons panko evenly over the tops of the 'shrooms. Using the back of a spatula, press down firmly on the mixture to create a nice compact patty.

4 In a large skillet over medium heat, warm 1 tablespoon of the olive oil until it shimmers. Gently flip the burgers, panko-cheese side down, into the pan, and cook until the cheese starts to get crispy, 3 to 4 minutes. Using a spatula, flip the 'shroom burgers and cook on the other side, until the caps are softened, 5 to 7 minutes. Lower the heat if necessary to prevent burning. If all the burgers do not fit in your skillet, repeat the process, using the remaining tablespoon olive oil.

5 Serve the burgers on buns with Hal's sauce, lettuce, and tomato.

Shake-
THEN-BAKE

CAULIFL

True to its name, shaking the cauliflower here coats it quickly and easily. I especially like this recipe because the coating isn't too heavy. In fact it's the perfect balance of veg to batter. I often turn these battered cauli bites into a meal by making them the star of a lettuce wrap. (Avocado and Hal's Everything Sauce, page 189, are great wingmen! Ha-ha!)

Serves
2 FOR A MEAL,
4 FOR A SIDE DISH

½ cup all-purpose flour

⅓ cup hot sauce (I like Frank's)

¼ cup unsweetened almond or oat milk

1 teaspoon garam masala

1 teaspoon fine sea salt

¼ teaspoon freshly ground black pepper

½ large head cauliflower, cored and broken into small florets (about 3 cups)

Butter lettuce leaves, avocado, fresh parsley, and Hal's Everything Sauce (page 189), for serving

 Preheat the oven to 425°F. Line a sheet pan with parchment paper. Set aside.

 In a large bowl with a tight-fitting lid, whisk the flour, hot sauce, almond milk, garam masala, salt, and pepper until smooth—the batter will be quite thick. Add the cauliflower, cover, and shake until the florets are well coated. If the florets don't coat evenly, use a rubber spatula to toss them some more. Using tongs or a fork, transfer the cauliflower to the prepared sheet pan, spreading out the florets so they are at least 1 inch apart. Bake for 15 minutes; then flip and bake until the batter starts to look crispy, another 10 to 15 minutes. (The thin batter that spreads out will get *very crispy* and is delicious, like the crispy parts of a grilled cheese!) If the florets haven't started to crisp (they don't really turn golden), raise the heat to 450°F if necessary for a few minutes.

 Wrap in butter lettuce with avocado and parsley and drizzle with Hal's sauce.

There's nothing like boxed mac and cheese. I mean, the process is incredible. Boil water, add dry noodles, strain, add butter, powder, stir. Voilà, instant meal. It just can't be beat. I wanted to replicate that method but improve the flavor, vegan or not. This mac powder is pleasingly cheesy tasting, and once made, it offers the convenience of a box, but better (and better for you).

Serves
1

⅔ cup elbow macaroni

1 tablespoon vegan butter or extra-virgin olive oil

1 teaspoon freshly squeezed lemon juice or vinegar

⅓ cup unsweetened almond or oat milk

3 tablespoons Mac Powder

Hot sauce, for serving (optional)

1 Cook the macaroni according to the package instructions. Strain the pasta and return it to the pot along with the butter and lemon juice.

2 Place the pot over low heat and stir until the butter has melted and the noodles are coated, then add the almond milk and Mac Powder and stir until thick, about 5 minutes. Remove from the heat, add a dash or two of hot sauce, if desired, and enjoy!

Mac Powder

MAKES ABOUT ½ CUP POWDER

In addition to using this to make Cheesy Vegan Mac, toast the powder and sprinkle it on popcorn or use it as a cheesy coating on tofu.

½ cup nutritional yeast

2 tablespoons all-purpose flour

2 teaspoons onion powder

1 teaspoon garlic powder

½ teaspoon fine sea salt

½ teaspoon organic cane sugar

¼ teaspoon white pepper

¼ teaspoon paprika

¼ teaspoon turmeric

In a blender, combine the yeast, flour, onion and garlic powders, salt, sugar, pepper, paprika, and turmeric. Pulse until well combined. Store in a jar or airtight container at room temp for up to 2 months.

EASY MEALS

FREEZER

My college **DORM ROOM** was no kitchen, but it had a *microwave*. At that time, about 80 percent of my diet was frozen *burritos*, which took 60 seconds on high to heat and required no utensils. Still, nothing is better to me at the end of a long day than a hot 'rito. These are a dupe of the **FROZEN** ones I used to buy. You can easily swap out the vegetables for ones you have on *hand*, from cooked carrots to leftover kale. These are great as a *breakfast* burrito, too. If you remember, move a 'rito from the freezer to the **FRIDGE** the night before to defrost. This cuts your reheating time in half.

Burri

Makes
6 TO 8 BURRITOS

2 tablespoons extra-virgin olive oil

1 teaspoon smoked paprika

1 teaspoon ground cumin

¼ teaspoon red pepper flakes

1 medium yellow onion, diced
(about 1½ cups)

¾ teaspoon fine sea salt, plus
more for seasoning

¼ teaspoon freshly ground black pepper,
plus more for seasoning

1 (15-ounce) can black beans,
drained and rinsed

7 ounces (about ½ block) firm tofu,
drained

1 (15-ounce) can diced fire-roasted
tomatoes, drained

1 sweet or baking potato, steamed
and cut into ¾-inch cubes (see Get
Steamy with Taters!, page 204)

8 (8- to 10-inch) flour tortillas

1 (5-ounce) bag baby spinach

2 cups cooked rice (optional)

2 cups vegan shredded
white cheese

1 In a medium skillet over medium-high heat, warm the olive oil until it starts to shimmer. Add the paprika, cumin, and pepper flakes and stir until the spices become fragrant, about 1 minute.

2 Lower the heat to medium, add the onion, sprinkle with a few pinches of the salt and the pepper, and cook, stirring, until softened, about 3 minutes. Add the drained beans, mashing them in the skillet with the back of a spatula or wooden spoon. Stir in the ¾ teaspoon salt and the ¼ teaspoon pepper. Continue to cook and stir, breaking up the beans until they become somewhat crispy and resemble ground beef, 13 to 15 minutes.

3 Next, crush the tofu between your fingers, add it to the skillet, and stir to combine with the beans. Continue cooking, stirring, to dry it out, 3 to 4 minutes. Next, add the tomatoes and potato cubes. Season everything again with a few pinches of salt and pepper. At this point I like to taste to make sure the mixture is seasoned properly, adjusting the spices if necessary. Continue to cook over medium heat, stirring occasionally, until everything is thoroughly combined, 5 to 8 minutes. Remove from the heat and let cool.

4 Next, grab a tortilla and a handful of spinach, spreading the leaves out in an even layer at the center of the wrap. Top with ¼ cup of the rice (if using) and about ¾ cup of the bean mixture, keeping it to the center of the tortilla. Sprinkle with 2 to 3 tablespoons of the cheese.

5 Fold up the bottom of the tortilla. Then fold in the sides toward the filling in the center, and roll from the bottom upward. Repeat with the remaining filling and wraps. Then wrap each burrito in foil, place the burritos in an airtight container, and freeze.

REHEAT YOUR 'RITO

Grab a frozen burrito, foil still on, and bake at 400°F for 25 to 30 minutes, or until heated through. Unwrap from one end and enjoy it like a Hot Pocket! For quicker heating: Take the foil completely off the burrito and wrap it with a damp paper towel. Place on a heat-safe plate and warm in the microwave for 2 to 3 minutes on high, or until it's heated through.

AND TOASTED QUINOA Kale SALAD

Serves
1 HUNGRY PERSON AS A MEAL OR 2 TO 4 AS A SIDE SALAD

2 cups chopped kale leaves

3 to 4 tablespoons Spicy Citrus Vinaigrette (page 190)

1 cup broccoli florets

½ cucumber, diced

2 tablespoons pitted and chopped black olives

¼ cup canned chickpeas, drained

¼ red onion, thinly sliced (about ¼ cup)

1 batch (1 cup) Savory Quinoa Crunch (page 227)

Fine sea salt and freshly ground black pepper, for seasoning

Toasting quinoa may hide its original flavor, but in my opinion, flavor is not what it's about. I'm in for the incredible *crunch!* Here I toss toasted quinoa with crispy kale and a tart, spicy vinaigrette so every forkful is perfectly balanced with crunch, some spice, and a generous amount of seasoning. The salad also stores really well in the fridge—I've eaten it over the course of three days. However, keep a portion of the quinoa aside to sprinkle on just before serving. In the fridge, crunchy quinoa becomes soft. I'm telling you, crunchy quinoa is here to stay.

1 Add the kale to a medium bowl and drizzle with 1 tablespoon of the Spicy Citrus Vinaigrette. Using your fingers, massage the dressing into the leaves until they soften. Next add the broccoli, cucumber, black olives, chickpeas, and red onion. Drizzle with another 2 to 3 tablespoons vinaigrette and toss until all the ingredients are well coated.

2 Right before eating, toss in ½ cup of the Savory Quinoa Crunch and sprinkle the remaining ½ cup over the top. Taste and add salt and pepper as needed. (Both the olives and the quinoa crunch lend some salty notes, so that's why I wait until the end of the process to season!)

4. The Sw

EETS

Section

·A· BIG

SLICE OF

I like to think this cake is **PERFECT** (or as perfect as things ever get), because unlike many *vegan* cakes, it requires no **special** methods or ingredients. In theory, this recipe is *foolproof* (I don't want to jinx it, though!). Wonderfully **SPONGY** and moist, this cake round, when divided into quarters, *stacked*, and covered with swirls of Old-Fashioned Frosting (page 158), can be quickly transformed into a *fun* extra-large slice of *birthday* cake for a few special friends or just you!

Frosted CAKE

Makes
1 EXTRA-LARGE
SLICE OF CAKE
(SERVES 1 OR SEVERAL)

Baking spray

1¾ cups all-purpose flour or all-purpose
gluten-free flour

½ cup tapioca starch or cornstarch

1 cup organic cane sugar

2 teaspoons baking powder

¼ teaspoon fine sea salt

1 cup unsweetened oat milk or
plant milk of choice

½ cup refined coconut oil, melted

1 prepared vegan Flax or Chia Egg
(page 198)

1 tablespoon pure vanilla extract

2 teaspoons white vinegar

Old-Fashioned Frosting (page 158)

1   Preheat the oven to 350°F. Lightly coat one 8-inch round cake pan with baking spray. Set aside.

2   In a medium bowl, whisk together the flour, tapioca starch, sugar, baking powder, and salt until combined. Add the oat milk, melted coconut oil, Flax Egg, vanilla, and vinegar. Stir until mostly smooth and fully combined.

3   Spread the batter evenly into the prepared pan (it will be thick). Bake until the top of the cake springs back when you gently touch it, or until a toothpick inserted into the cake comes out clean and the edges turn golden, about 45 minutes. Transfer the pan to a rack to cool. After 10 minutes, turn the cake over onto a rack or a sheet pan and let cool completely. Frost (see below) or eat as is.

4   *How to assemble a Big Slice:* Level the top of your cake with a serrated knife by gently slicing off any dome that may have developed while baking. Cut the cake into quarters to get four equal-size pieces.

5   Spread 1 to 2 tablespoons of frosting on the first piece. Top that with a second piece, frost that, and repeat until all four pieces are stacked. Push a straw or skewer cut to be just slightly shorter than the stacked cake layers down through the entire stack to keep your big slice standing straight. Spread the remaining frosting on the sides and top of the cake. Use the back of a spoon to create swirls if desired.

☆ Keep It Round and Top It Off

Instead of making one big slice, sometimes I like to keep the cake round. I cut the round in half horizontally and spread Mixed Berry Chia Jam (page 223, but double the recipe) between the two layers, pile the top high with cut-up mixed berries, and dollop with Magic Vegan Whip (page 229).

Old-Fashioned Frosting

MAKES ENOUGH TO FROST AN 8-INCH ROUND OR A BIG SLICE OF FROSTED CAKE (PAGE 154)

I've always had trouble frosting cakes. It's most likely because I'm impatient and don't wait for the cakes to cool properly, so be sure your cake layers are completely cooled. (I like to put them in the freezer to cool. I'm not kidding when I say I'm impatient.) This frosting uses an old-fashioned method of cooking the base, which feels a lot like pudding before you add the vegan butter. The result is light, almost marshmallowy, and not too sweet. You do need a hand mixer for this recipe. If you don't have one, they are relatively inexpensive, and worth the investment for this recipe alone because it's that good.

½ cup unsweetened oat milk or plant milk of choice

½ cup organic cane sugar

¼ cup all-purpose flour

½ cup vegan butter, softened to room temperature

1 teaspoon pure vanilla extract

Pinch of fine sea salt

Pinch of ground cinnamon (optional)

In a medium saucepan over medium heat, combine the oat milk, sugar, and flour. Whisk constantly until smooth, about 3 minutes. Continue to whisk the mixture until it becomes pudding-like, about another 3 minutes. (It will become difficult to whisk the thicker it gets, but just keep going!)

Remove the pan from the heat and let the mixture sit for 10 to 15 minutes before transferring it to a sealable container and chilling it in the fridge for at least an hour, or until completely cool.

Add the butter to a medium bowl, and using a hand mixer, whip until it's light in color.

Remove the cooled flour mixture from the fridge and spoon it into the whipped butter a few tablespoons at a time, mixing well with the hand mixer after each addition. Add the vanilla, salt, and the cinnamon (if using) and whip for another 2 minutes on high.

Store in the fridge until ready to use.

Lemon or Chocolate Old-Fashioned Frosting

Add 1 to 2 teaspoons finely grated lemon zest when you add the vanilla or ¼ cup melted and cooled (but still liquid) semi-sweet vegan chocolate chips for different flavor frostings.

FUNFETTI Cake FOR ONE

Am I allowed to put a recipe in a headnote? Why not? It goes with the story. My grandpa taught me a recipe for what he called 3-2-1 Cake. All it takes is a gallon freezer bag, a box of angel food cake mix, a box of vanilla cake mix, and a quick shake. Whenever I wanted cake, he told me all I had to do was scoop 3 tablespoons of the gallon-bag mix into a greased mug, add 2 tablespoons of milk or water, stir, and microwave for one minute. When I was little, it was perfect, because I didn't have great cake recipes to compare this concoction to, and it was sweet enough for me not to care. Now I recognize the beauty of a mug cake, but need for it to taste as good as a freshly baked one from the oven. So here, a very fun 1-4-2-2-1-½-¼-¼ cake for Grandpa Dutchie.

Serves
1

1 heaping tablespoon refined coconut oil

4 tablespoons all-purpose flour

2 tablespoons oat milk or plant-based milk of choice

2 tablespoons organic cane sugar

1 tablespoon vegan sprinkles

½ teaspoon pure vanilla extract

¼ teaspoon baking powder

¼ teaspoon white vinegar

1 In a large mug, melt the coconut oil in the microwave on high for 15 to 30 seconds. Swirl the mug to coat the sides with the oil. Add the flour, oat milk, sugar, sprinkles, vanilla, baking powder, and vinegar into the mug and stir just until mostly smooth. Using the back of the spoon, spread the top of the batter evenly.

2 Microwave until the cake has become fluffy and the top is set (if you press it with your finger, no indentation should appear, or it should spring back immediately), or 1 minute 30 seconds. If an indentation appears, microwave in 15-second intervals until a toothpick inserted into the cake comes out dry. Enjoy immediately.

Chocolate Whip

SERVES 2

Avocado has a certain creamy quality that makes for the silkiest, most airy dessert. This recipe is perfectly portioned for two and has a milk-chocolate-like flavor through and through. If you're looking for something a little cooler, try freezing this whip. It makes a great soft serve.

2 avocados, halved and pitted

½ cup Instant Plant Milk (page 199) or unsweetened oat milk

½ cup unsweetened cocoa powder

¼ cup maple syrup

Magic Vegan Whip (page 229), for serving (optional)

Scoop the pulp of both avocados into a blender. Then add the plant milk, cocoa powder, and maple syrup. Pulse, scraping down the sides of the blender as needed, until the mixture is completely smooth. Divide between two small dessert bowls and chill in the fridge for at least 2 hours before enjoying.

Top with Magic Vegan Whip, if desired.

Raspberry Whip

SERVES 2

Silken tofu is the underdog of tofu varieties. It is light in texture and flavor and pairs brilliantly with tart raspberries. The texture of this treat is similar to a smooth chia pudding.

4 ounces (about ¼ package) silken tofu, drained

1 cup fresh or frozen raspberries

1 tablespoon freshly squeezed lemon juice

1 to 2 tablespoons maple syrup

1 teaspoon ground chia seeds

Magic Vegan Whip (page 229), for serving (optional)

In a blender, combine the tofu, raspberries, lemon juice, 1 tablespoon of the maple syrup, and the chia seeds. Blend on high until the mixture is completely smooth, scraping down the sides as needed. Place a fine-mesh sieve over a bowl and push the blended mixture through it to remove the raspberry seeds. Taste and add the remaining 1 tablespoon maple syrup, if desired. Divide the de-seeded mixture between two small dessert bowls and chill in the fridge for at least 2 hours before enjoying.

Top with Magic Vegan Whip, if desired.

CLASSIC Chocolate Chip COOKIES

(The Only Vegan Cookie Recipe You Need!)

Makes
10 TO 12 CHOCOLATE CHUNK COOKIES

¼ cup vegan butter

¼ cup organic cane sugar

¼ cup organic light brown sugar

1 (5-ounce) vegan dark chocolate bar, chopped (to make 1 scant cup)

1 cup all-purpose flour

¼ teaspoon baking soda

½ teaspoon coarse sea salt

1 prepared Flax Egg (page 198)

2 teaspoons white vinegar

½ teaspoon pure vanilla extract

Baking and I have a weird relationship. As much as I appreciate a recipe, I tend to experiment when making food. I've found that when it comes to vegan baking, though, experimentation doesn't always work in my favor. After countless recipe tests (and fails), I've combined and tweaked a few of the internet's vegan cookie recipes to produce a failproof cookie recipe that needs no adjustments, only additions if you want to change the flavor (see A Cookie for Any Craving, page 162). For this version, I like to chop up whatever my favorite chocolate bar is at the time for a chocolate chunk cookie that is soft yet well-structured, and just the right amount of sweet.

 Preheat the oven to 350°F. Cover a sheet pan with parchment paper. Set aside.

 In a small saucepan over medium heat, combine the butter and sugars, stirring constantly just until the mixture becomes smooth. Remove from the heat and let cool slightly.

 In a large bowl, stir together the chocolate chunks, flour, baking soda, and ¼ teaspoon of the salt.

(recipe continues)

4 Next, stir in the cooled butter-sugar mixture, Flax Egg, vinegar, and vanilla and stir to form a dough. You may want to use your hands to bring the dough together, almost kneading it to ensure all the dry ingredients are moistened and combined, working it just until the dough is completely smooth and soft.

5 Using a tablespoon, scoop out heaping portions of dough and form 10 to 12 (2-inch) balls. Place them 2 inches apart on the lined sheet pan. (You may need a second sheet pan if you ended up with 12 cookies.) Sprinkle with the remaining salt and bake until the cookies just start to turn golden on the edges, about 15 minutes. Remove from the oven and let cool before enjoying.

A COOKIE FOR ANY CRAVING

1 **Sugar Cookies:** Omit the chocolate chunks in the recipe and roll unbaked cookie balls in cane sugar before baking.

2 **Snickerdoodles:** Omit the chocolate chunks in the recipe and stir together 1 tablespoon sugar and 1 teaspoon ground cinnamon. Roll unbaked cookie balls in the mixture and bake as directed.

3 **Berry Good Cookies:** Omit the chocolate chunks in the recipe. Toss ½ cup fresh berries or frozen berries with 1 tablespoon flour and gently work them into the fully prepared dough before forming cookie balls. Bake as directed.

4 **Soft-Baked Choco-Banana Cookies:** Substitute ¼ cup mashed banana for the prepared Flax Egg and add 2 tablespoons of your favorite plant milk. Otherwise make the cookies as directed.

COOL

Mint

PATTIES

If I could wish myself into a state of being, it would be the experience of a person in a York Peppermint Patty commercial—feeling a gust of wind blow in my face as I bite into a cool, chocolaty mint. These smooth and rich patties are a homemade version on the cusp of perfection. The only thing missing are the sound effects, a camera crew with a fan, and studio lighting.

Makes
5 (2½-INCH) PATTIES

1 cup organic confectioners' sugar, plus more for rolling out

2 tablespoons vegan butter or refined coconut oil

½ teaspoon peppermint extract

For the coating

½ cup vegan dark chocolate chips

1 teaspoon refined coconut oil

1 candy cane, or 2 to 3 peppermint candies, crushed

 1 Line a plate, small sheet pan, or freezer-safe dish with parchment paper. Set aside.

 2 In a medium bowl, stir together the confectioners' sugar, vegan butter, and peppermint extract until a smooth dough is formed. (If you are having trouble getting the dough smooth, it may be easier to use your hands to bring the dough together.)

 3 Lightly sprinkle your work surface with confectioners' sugar, and using your fingers, press the dough into a 4 × 7-inch rectangle that's about ¼ inch thick. (You can also use a rolling pin, but fingers work just fine.) Using a 2½-inch round cup or cookie cutter, cut out as many circles as you can.

 4 Bring together any leftover dough into a ball and repeat the process of making a dough rectangle and cutting out the circles until all (or at least most) of the dough is used. Place the mint patties onto the prepared plate and freeze until solid, 1 to 2 hours.

 5 *When the patties are frozen, make the coating:* In a microwave-safe dish, combine the chocolate chips and coconut oil and zap for 30 seconds. Remove the chocolate mixture from the microwave and stir until smooth. If the chocolate is not completely melted, zap for another 10 seconds. Repeat this step, stirring and zapping, until the mixture is completely smooth. Let cool, stirring often, for about 10 minutes.

 6 Remove the mint patties from the freezer, and one by one, using a fork, lower each patty into the chocolate, fully coating it and letting the excess drip off. Return the coated patty to the parchment paper. Repeat with the remaining patties. Sprinkle the coated patties with a few pinches of crushed candy cane.

 7 Return the chocolate-coated patties to the freezer until they are fully frozen again and the chocolate becomes hard, another 10 to 20 minutes. Enjoy straight from the freezer. Store in a resealable bag or plastic container in the freezer for up to 1 month.

Fruit PUDDLES

When I bite into something covered with chocolate, I want the inside to be surprising and satisfying, like these puddles, which are dark on the outside and give no clue to what's inside, which is—spoiler alert—a fruity, creamy center. This sweet doesn't require too much thought (or many ingredients), but it does take a little patience while you wait for the treat to freeze.

Makes
6 TO 8 PUDDLES

½ cup unsweetened soy-based yogurt, such as Silk

1 cup frozen mixed berries, slightly thawed

For the coating
½ cup vegan chocolate chips

1 teaspoon refined coconut oil

 In a blender, combine the yogurt and frozen fruit and pulse until smooth.

 Line a flat plate or freezer-safe dish with parchment paper, and using a spoon or small ice cream scoop, dollop "puddles" of the yogurt-fruit mixture onto the prepared plate or dish. Place the puddles in the freezer until they are hardened through, 1 to 2 hours.

 When the puddles are frozen, make the coating: In a microwave-safe dish, combine the chocolate chips and coconut oil and zap for 30 seconds.

 Remove the chocolate mixture from the microwave and stir until smooth. If the chocolate has not completely melted, zap for another 10 seconds. Repeat this step, stirring and zapping, until the mixture is completely smooth. Let cool, stirring often, for about 10 minutes.

5 Remove the puddles from the freezer. Peel one puddle at a time off the paper, and using a spoon, lower the puddle into the chocolate, fully coating it and letting the excess drip off. Return the coated puddle to the parchment paper. Repeat with the remaining puddles. Return the chocolate-coated puddles to the freezer until they are fully frozen again and the chocolate becomes hard, another 10 to 20 minutes. Enjoy straight from the freezer. Store in a resealable bag or plastic container in the freezer for up to 1 month.

These are the result of the inventive cooking I used to do in my college dorm room. The crunchy bites were dope because (a) they taste amazing; (b) I could steal the cornflakes from the dining hall cereal dispensers and needed only a few more ingredients; and (c) I could store them in the freezer compartment of my mini fridge. Ideally every recipe would use six ingredients or less, but the world is imperfect, and besides, if that were the case, recipes like this would stop seeming so convenient. Lucky for us, recipes can still be easy, and this is the beauty of Cornflake Butterfingers (and of course, the first reason above, too).

Makes
8 BARS

2½ cups cornflakes

1 cup creamy or crunchy peanut butter or nut butter of choice

2 tablespoons Cheap & Sweet Syrup (page 194) or maple syrup

For the coating
½ cup vegan chocolate chips

1 teaspoon refined coconut oil

1 Put 2 cups of the cornflakes into a blender and pulse on high until pulverized into a fine flour. Transfer the cornflake flour to a medium bowl (you should have about ½ cup flour) and add the peanut butter and Cheap & Sweet Syrup. Stir until smooth and well combined. Fold the remaining ½ cup cornflakes into the dough for extra crunch.

2 Place the dough ball onto a piece of parchment paper, and top with a second piece of parchment. Using your hands or a rolling pin, press or roll the mixture into a 6 × 8-inch square that's about ¼ inch thick. Pull the edges of the parchment up along the sides of the square to form clean edges.

3 **Make the coating:** In a microwave-safe dish, combine the chocolate chips and coconut oil and zap for 30 seconds. Remove the chocolate mixture from the microwave and stir until smooth. If the chocolate has not completely melted, zap for another 10 seconds. Repeat this step, stirring and zapping, until the mixture is completely smooth. Let cool, stirring often, for about 10 minutes.

4 Pour the cooled chocolate over the cornflake–peanut butter square, and using an offset spatula or the back of a spoon, spread it out smoothly in an even layer.

5 Put the coated cornflake square in the freezer until the chocolate coating has hardened, about 20 minutes. Cut into 2 × 3-inch bars and serve. If you have any left over (I never do), store in the freezer for up to 1 month.

CORNFLAKE BUTTERFINGERS

FRUIT PUDDLES
(PAGE 166)

CORNFLAKE
BUTTERFINGERS
(PAGE 167)

COOL MINT PATTIES
(PAGE 164)

Two-Ingredient ICE CREAM

(NO BANANAS!)

Vegan ice cream isn't ice cream unless it's creamy, which I've discovered isn't always the case with dairy-free recipes and store-bought vegan options. While frozen bananas make for an icy, sweet substitute, I find they are a little over-powering when they are used as an ice cream base. This recipe is decadent and smooth without a banana base, and the flavor can easily be adjusted to your preferences by swapping out the frozen berries for other frozen fruits.

Makes
ABOUT 1 PINT

¾ cup Vegan Condensed Milk (page 202) or condensed coconut milk

3 cups frozen raspberries or other frozen fruit

 In a blender, combine the Vegan Condensed Milk and the frozen berries. Blend on high until completely smooth, scraping down the sides of the blender as needed.

 Transfer the ice cream to a freezer-safe container with a top, cover, and freeze overnight. Let thaw for 5 to 10 minutes before serving.

SOUR

Sour straws are one of my *favorite* candies. They are tart, chewy, and **STRETCHY**. With rice paper and fresh fruit, you can make your own version at *home*. Feel free to change up the fruit. Maybe mango? Possibly raspberry? And the smaller the dice, the thinner the straw. To **CRUSH** the freeze-dried fruit, I put a few pieces in a *plastic* baggie and smash it with a rolling pin. It's like a homemade candy coating, and it adds a **pop** of **COLOR** to this homemade sweet.

Straws

Makes
4 TO 6 STRAWS

2 to 3 round rice paper sheets

¼ cup water

2 tablespoons freshly squeezed lemon juice

2 tablespoons organic cane sugar

1 teaspoon crushed freeze-dried strawberries

½ cup finely diced strawberries

1 Using kitchen shears, cut two of the rice paper sheets in half so you get 4 half circles.

2 On a large rimmed dinner plate, combine the water and lemon juice. On a separate plate, stir together the sugar and freeze-dried strawberries.

3 Dip one half-circle rice paper sheet in the lemon-water mixture for 5 seconds, then lay the rice paper sheet flat on the counter or workspace with the straight edge toward you. Using your hands, place a line of diced strawberries about a thumb-width in (you want to have enough paper to fold over the fruit and seal it in before you start rolling) and parallel to the straight edge of the rice paper. Try to seal the fruit in as tightly as you can. Next, roll the sealed fruit away from you, pulling the wrapper taut as you go, until it is fully rolled into a straw. Pinch the ends together to hold the filling, or you can even twist them.

4 Roll the straw in the sugar–dried fruit mixture until well coated. Repeat with the remaining rice paper sheets, cutting the third sheet if you have more filling to use. Enjoy immediately.

Banana Crunch

Rice cakes aren't as plain as they seem—sometimes they just need reinvention. For example, grind them up and they make a great coating on these banana crunch bites. The ground-up puffed rice gives an airiness that I feel is similar to that of a Ferrero Rocher chocolate. I like to think of these as Peanut Butter Banana Rochers.

Makes
ABOUT 14 BITES

3 plain rice cakes, or more as needed

⅓ cup creamy peanut butter (see **Not All Peanut Butters Are Created Equal, page 177**) or other spread of choice, such as cocoa spread

2 bananas, peeled, cut into 1-inch pieces, and frozen

For the coating
⅓ cup vegan chocolate chips

1 tablespoon refined coconut oil

1 Line a tray or small sheet pan that will fit in your freezer with parchment paper. Set aside.

2 Add the rice cakes to a blender or food processor and pulse on high until a powder forms. Transfer the rice powder to a plate.

3 In the microwave, heat the peanut butter until it becomes thin enough for dipping into, starting with 20 seconds, stirring, then heating until it's a nice melty consistency. Alternately, you can melt it in a double boiler on the stovetop, stirring constantly until it's thin enough for dipping,

4 Remove the frozen banana pieces from the freezer, and using a fork or Popsicle stick, dip one of the frozen pieces into the thinned peanut butter until fully coated. Then roll the banana in the ground rice powder until it's fully covered. Place it on the prepared tray or sheet pan. Repeat until all the frozen banana pieces are coated. Freeze for 1 hour.

BITES

5 *After the peanut-butter-covered bananas are frozen, make the coating:* In a microwave-safe dish, combine the chocolate chips and coconut oil and zap for 30 seconds.

6 Remove the chocolate mixture from the microwave and stir until smooth. If the chocolate has not completely melted, zap for another 10 seconds. Repeat this step, stirring and zapping, until the mixture is completely smooth. Let cool, stirring often, for about 10 minutes.

7 Remove the bananas from the freezer, and again, using a fork or Popsicle stick, dip each frozen banana in the melted chocolate and roll in a second layer of rice powder to create a stronger, crunchier shell. If you need more rice powder, grind up another rice cake or two as needed. Freeze for 2 hours before enjoying.

8 Store in a freezer-safe resealable container or resealable freezer bag for up to 1 week. Always enjoy from the freezer.

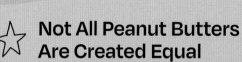

☆ Not All Peanut Butters Are Created Equal

Sometimes I stare at the grocery store peanut butter shelf in awe. There are so many choices: conventional, natural, creamy, crunchy, organic, not organic. For my Banana Crunch Bites, you want to reach for regular, oil-added creamy peanut butter, such as Jif or Skippy. The addition of palm or soybean oil makes it melt much better than a natural peanut butter, which can get grainy.

GRANOLA *Cheesecake*

This freezer cheesecake is a combination of my Magic Vegan Whip with cream cheese (even better with my Tofu Cream Cheese, page 205). It makes for a fluffy, creamy filling that has the lightness and cheesy flavor of a non-vegan recipe. When I want a thick crust and a high layer of filling (which I often do), I use a smaller dish. Using an 8-inch square pan, like the one called for in this recipe, results in a slice that resembles a typical bar, like a brownie. You can also try filling an ice cube tray with crust and filling, and enjoy a two-bite cheesecake whenever you have a hankering.

Makes
16 BARS

For the crust

1 recipe unbaked Go-To Baked Granola (page 222)

For the filling

1 cup Tofu Cream Cheese (page 205) or vegan cream cheese, such as Kite Hill

3 tablespoons organic cane sugar

1 teaspoon pure vanilla extract

¾ cup whipped Magic Vegan Whip (page 229) or heavy whipping cream alternative, such as Silk Dairy Free, whipped to soft peaks

 Preheat the oven to 350°F. Line an 8-inch square pan with parchment, leaving a 1-inch overhang on two sides. Set aside.

 Make the crust: Press the unbaked granola evenly into the prepared pan, trying to eliminate any spaces between the mixture. Bake until the granola is fragrant and the edges just start to turn golden, about 20 minutes. Let cool.

 Meanwhile, make the filling: In a medium bowl, using a hand mixer, whip the Tofu Cream Cheese, sugar, and vanilla until smooth, then gently fold in the Magic Vegan Whip.

 Spread the mixture evenly onto the cooled crust and cover with plastic wrap. Freeze for at least 2 hours before cutting into 2 × 2-inch squares. Enjoy frozen. Store in the freezer in a lidded container for up to 1 week.

 ## Three-Ingredient No-Fuss Crust

If you are short on ingredients, try replacing the granola crust with this quick and easy option. In a bowl, stir together 1¼ cups vegan graham cracker crumbs, 5 tablespoons melted vegan butter, and 3 tablespoons organic cane sugar until well combined. Line an 8-inch square pan with parchment, leaving a 1-inch overhang on two sides, and bake at 350°F until it starts to turn golden on the edges and becomes fragrant, about 25 minutes. Use for Granola Cheesecake Bars.

·A· SMALL

Pie

CALL ME VEGAN

Makes
1 SMALL PIE

2 tablespoons refined coconut oil, plus more for coating

6 tablespoons all-purpose flour, plus more for rolling out

1 tablespoon organic cane sugar

Pinch of fine sea salt

2 tablespoons cold water

¼ to ⅓ cup Mixed Berry Chia Jam (page 223), or store-bought jam with 1 teaspoon chia seeds stirred in

Sometimes you need a homemade sweet just for you (or you and a friend). If you are having such a craving (or you need to use up your Mixed Berry Chia Jam, page 223), this recipe is for you. Plus, a small pie means fewer ingredients—and less dedication to finishing a dessert you might not want the next day. One scoop of dairy-free ice cream fits perfectly atop this pie, and the small size means you can make another dessert tomorrow, since you'll most likely be finishing this in one night.

1 Preheat the oven to 400°F. Lightly coat a 3½-to-4-inch ramekin with coconut oil. Set aside.

2 In a small bowl, using a fork, stir together the flour, sugar, and salt. Add the 2 tablespoons of coconut oil, and with the fork, break it up in the flour mixture to make pea-sized balls. Sprinkle the water over the flour-oil mixture and stir to form a smooth dough. Sprinkle your work surface lightly with flour and divide the dough ball into two pieces, one double the size of the other. Roll out the larger piece to a 5-inch circle (or one that just fits into your dish) and transfer to the prepared ramekin. Spoon the Mixed Berry Chia Jam into the crust-lined ramekin.

3 Sprinkle your surface again with flour and roll out the remaining dough to a 4-inch circle, or one that is just about the diameter of your ramekin. Cut the circle into ¾-inch strips and arrange them on top of your pie in a woven pattern. Using a knife, trim any excess dough that overhangs the ramekin.

4 Bake until the crust is golden brown all over and the jam is bubbling under the crust, 35 to 40 minutes. Let cool for at least 15 minutes before removing from the ramekin and serving.

5. VEG

B

AN

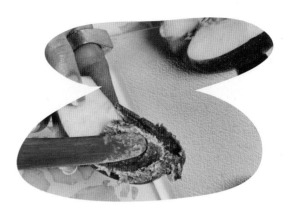

ASICS

ONE WEEK'S WORTH OF Sushi Rice

I love this recipe because it takes care of 50 percent of my meals for the week. Leftover takeout? I heat up some of this tasty sticky rice to go along with it. Cucumber Bites (page 37)? I'm ready to go. Crispy Rice Balls (page 118)? I can make them in minutes. With patience and an eye on the clock, you can whip up a batch of this weekly staple in just under an hour.

Makes
5 TO 7 DAYS' WORTH OF RICE (OR 12 CUPS)

5¼ cups water, plus more for rinsing

4 cups sushi rice

⅔ cup rice vinegar

2 tablespoons maple syrup or organic cane sugar

2 tablespoons soy sauce

1. Rinse the rice in cold water until it runs clear. In a large pot over high heat, combine the rice and the 5¼ cups water. Bring the water to a boil, then reduce the heat to low so the rice cooks at a slow simmer. Cover and let cook for 12 to 15 minutes. Remove the pot from the heat.

2. In a medium microwave-safe bowl, combine the vinegar, maple syrup, and soy sauce. Heat for 30 seconds. Stir until well combined (or the sugar has dissolved). Pour the mixture over the cooked rice and stir to combine. Cover the rice with a damp towel until cool.

3. Divide the rice into sealable containers for 5 to 7 days of meals and store in the fridge.

Makes
2 CUPS

1 cup nutritional yeast

1 cup panko bread crumbs or
gluten-free panko bread crumbs

2 tablespoons onion powder

2 tablespoons garlic powder

2 tablespoons dried parsley

2 tablespoons dried oregano

2 tablespoons dried basil

2 tablespoons poppy seeds

2 tablespoons sesame seeds

1 tablespoon fine sea salt

1 tablespoon white pepper

1 teaspoon red pepper flakes

I wish I could make a hundred jars of this stuff to have on hand because I truly use it on EVERYTHING. It has changed my life. Since this seasoning mix combines bread crumbs and nutritional yeast, it has a cheesy, toasted flavor that enhances most anything savory. It also works as a coating that gets crispy in an oven or air fryer. Make sure you blend the mixture into a fine powder—this step ensures that it sticks to anything and everything. Feel free to use gluten-free bread crumbs. I hope it, too, becomes your spice cabinet favorite.

1 In a blender or food processor, combine the yeast, bread crumbs, onion and garlic powders, parsley, oregano, basil, poppy and sesame seeds, salt, white pepper, and pepper flakes and pulse until the mixture turns into a fine powder.

2 Store in an airtight container or lidded mason jar for up to 4 months.

Hal's EVERYTHING Seasoning

Hal's EVERYTHING Sauce

Makes
ABOUT ⅔ CUP

¼ cup Homemade Vegan Mayo (page 196) or store-bought vegan mayo

1 tablespoon Dijon mustard

1 tablespoon barbecue sauce

1 tablespoon ketchup

1 tablespoon maple syrup

Juice from ½ lemon

2 teaspoons sriracha

1 teaspoon minced garlic

1 teaspoon dried parsley

Pinch of fine sea salt

Freshly ground black pepper

A beautiful pairing with Hal's Everything Seasoning, this sauce is a combination of a few of my favorite vegan fast-food sauces. The flavor is basically a mix of everything.

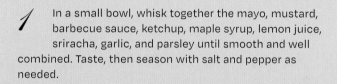 In a small bowl, whisk together the mayo, mustard, barbecue sauce, ketchup, maple syrup, lemon juice, sriracha, garlic, and parsley until smooth and well combined. Taste, then season with salt and pepper as needed.

 Store in the fridge in a lidded jar or container for up to 1 week.

SPICY *Citrus* VINAIGRETTE

 Makes
1¼ CUPS

½ cup extra-virgin olive oil or avocado oil

Juice from 1 large orange (about ⅓ cup) or the equivalent from another citrus fruit, like lemons or grapefruit

¼ cup water

1 to 2 tablespoons maple syrup, depending on desired sweetness

2 chipotle peppers in adobo sauce

½ teaspoon dried oregano

½ teaspoon freshly ground black pepper

½ teaspoon garlic powder

¼ teaspoon fine sea salt

This dressing is hot in more ways than one. The beauty of warming this already spicy vinaigrette is that it can turn a cool salad into a comforting meal on a cold night. When you reduce it (see Get Saucy! below), the flavor intensifies and becomes, if you will, clingier (in a good way, not like a bad relationship). But don't get me wrong, it's just as delicious cold. The peppers give the dressing a nice kick, balanced out by the sweetness of the citrus and maple. I buy greens in bulk to eat my way through during the week, so having this already-made dressing makes salad prep ten times easier.

1 In a blender, combine the olive oil, orange juice, water, maple syrup, chipotle peppers, oregano, pepper, garlic powder, and salt. Blend on high until smooth. If serving warm, heat in the microwave on high for 1 minute before using.

2 Store in a lidded jar or container for up to 1 week.

 ## Get Saucy!

I like to douse a reduced version of this dressing on Smashed Sprouts (page 52), or pretty much any roasted vegetable. Warm the vinaigrette in a small saucepan over medium-high heat until it comes to a boil. Lower the heat slightly and continue to simmer, stirring occasionally, until the dressing reduces to the desired consistency. I like to simmer ¾ cup dressing down to ½ to ⅓ of a cup for a thickened glaze.

Balsamic

Because it can be somewhat pricey, knowing how to cook this thick, rich, and glossy vinegar reduction is like learning how to create liquid gold. Once you see how easy it is to make, you'll likely keep it on hand at all times. It's become a pantry staple for me. The sweet, tart, and savory notes complement everything from salads to fruits, toasted breads to roasted vegetables. It's great for gifts, too.

Makes
⅓ CUP

1 cup balsamic vinegar

¼ cup organic light brown sugar

1 In a small saucepan over medium heat, combine the vinegar and sugar. Bring the mixture to a slow boil, stirring occasionally, and after the sugar has dissolved, reduce the heat to low. Continue to simmer until the liquid thickens, stirring as needed, and has reduced to ⅓ cup, about 20 minutes.

2 Remove from the heat. Once cool, store in a jar for up to 3 weeks.

Juice It Up!

Try adding a bit of pomegranate juice or other fruit juice to customize your glaze!

GLAZE

Ranchy DRESSING

Makes
ABOUT 1½ CUPS

Large handful (about 1 cup) of fresh herbs, such as parsley, dill, basil, and/or oregano

½ cup oats, cashews, or sunflower seeds, soaked in water to cover overnight and drained

¼ cup water

¼ cup unsweetened soy-based yogurt, such as Silk

2 tablespoons freshly squeezed lemon juice

2 teaspoons nutritional yeast

2 teaspoons dried dill

1 teaspoon minced garlic

1 teaspoon onion powder

¼ teaspoon red pepper flakes

¼ teaspoon fine sea salt

Since there are so many dressings and dips to choose from nowadays, I wish I could say I've outgrown my obsession with ranch, but I haven't. There's just something about the creaminess and herbiness of this classic dressing that can't be beat. This dairy-free version is simple and good for you, plus it has a shorter ingredient list than most store-bought bottled options.

 In a blender, combine the herbs, oats, water, yogurt, lemon juice, nutritional yeast, dill, garlic, onion powder, pepper flakes, and salt. Process on high until smooth.

 Enjoy with fresh veggies right away, or store in a lidded jar or airtight container in the fridge for up to 2 weeks.

☆ No Time to Soak?

Soaking oats, nuts, or seeds overnight helps ensure a creamier texture when blending. (It also reduces the phytic acid in nuts and seeds, which can cause indigestion.) You can cut the soak time short by covering the grains, nuts, or seeds with boiling water and letting them steep for 30 minutes.

Before you ask any questions, make this savory version of my Cheap & Sweet Syrup (page 194). You'll see why this rich sauce is a Vegan Basics necessity. The salty umami of soy and the sweetness of sugar work well to create a syrup or glaze for Baby Carrot Fries (page 50) or Cucumber Bites (page 37). You can also use it in place of balsamic on toast topped with a thick slice of heirloom tomato or a dollop of mashed avocado, or drizzle it on fruit with a pinch of salt.

Makes
A SCANT ½ CUP

⅓ cup water plus ¼ teaspoon

¼ cup organic cane sugar

¼ cup organic light brown sugar

1 tablespoon soy sauce

½ teaspoon refined coconut oil

¼ teaspoon tapioca starch

1 teaspoon pure vanilla extract

1 In a small saucepan over medium-high heat, combine the ⅓ cup water, the cane and brown sugars, soy sauce, and coconut oil. Bring the mixture to a rolling boil; then reduce the heat and continue to cook at a slow simmer. In a small bowl, whisk together the ¼ teaspoon water and the tapioca starch until smooth. Then whisk this into the sugar mixture. Continue to whisk and cook until the mixture becomes syrupy and thick and has reduced to just under ½ cup, about 10 minutes. Stir in the vanilla.

2 Use immediately or let cool before transferring to a glass jar and storing in the fridge for up to 2 weeks.

Cheap & SWEET

When I post a recipe online calling for sweetener, I often get asked "What can I use in place of honey?" You'd think maple syrup would be the obvious vegan solution, but the thin consistency and strong flavor make it an inferior substitute in most recipes. Here's a homemade sweet syrup that has the same viscosity and dark golden color of a buckwheat or manuka honey, without the bees.

Makes
A SCANT 1 CUP

⅔ cup water plus ½ teaspoon

½ cup organic cane sugar

½ cup organic light brown sugar

1 teaspoon vegan butter or refined coconut oil

½ teaspoon tapioca starch

1 teaspoon pure vanilla extract

1 In a small saucepan over medium-high heat, combine the ⅔ cup water, the cane and brown sugars, and vegan butter. Bring the mixture to a rolling boil; then reduce the heat and continue to cook at a gentle simmer. In a small bowl, whisk together the ½ teaspoon water and the tapioca starch until smooth. Then whisk this into the sugar mixture. Continue to whisk and cook until the mixture becomes syrupy and thick and has reduced to just under a cup, about 10 minutes. Stir in the vanilla.

2 Use immediately or let cool before transferring to a glass jar and storing in the fridge for up to 2 weeks.

SYRUP

Homemade VEGAN MAYO

You won't believe how easy it is to make your own mayonnaise. And, I have to say, the eggless version might just be better than the original. While this spread is a perfect mayo substitute, it also works as a creamy addition to soups, sauces, and dips. The key here is to make sure all your ingredients are room temp, and to go very slowly when adding the oil. I am not kidding when I say go teaspoon by teaspoon. The mixture needs time to emulsify; otherwise you will find yourself with a soupy mess. For a thicker mayo, add another tablespoon or two of oil (slowly as well!).

Makes
½ CUP

¼ cup unsweetened soy milk, at room temp (or microwave cold soy milk for 20 seconds to warm it)

1 tablespoon freshly squeezed lemon juice or white vinegar

⅛ teaspoon fine sea salt

½ cup avocado oil, at room temperature

 In a blender, combine the milk, lemon juice, and salt. Add the oil 1 teaspoon at a time, blending on low for 20 seconds after each addition. The mixture should thicken after each addition. By the time you add the final teaspoon, your mayonnaise should be creamy and spreadable.

2 Store in the fridge in a lidded jar or container for up to 1 week.

Pickle MAYO

Makes
½ CUP

½ cup Homemade Vegan Mayo (page 196)
or store-bought vegan mayo

1 tablespoon white vinegar

1 teaspoon dried dill

¼ teaspoon paprika

⅛ teaspoon onion powder

⅛ teaspoon freshly ground black pepper

The addition of dill and vinegar to my homemade mayo base adds a tangy flavor that in my opinion can upgrade most any meal.

 In a small bowl, stir together the mayo, vinegar, dill, paprika, onion powder, and pepper.

 Store in the fridge in a lidded jar or container for up to 1 week.

Spicy MAYO

Makes
A GENEROUS ⅓ CUP

¼ cup Homemade Vegan Mayo (page 196)
or store-bought vegan mayo

2 tablespoons sriracha

1 tablespoon maple syrup

Spice up your mayo and use as an accompaniment to my Watermelon Tuna Bowl (page 114) or to kick up your potato salad a notch. It's good in dips and wraps, too.

 In a small bowl, stir together the mayo, sriracha, and maple syrup until smooth.

 Store in the fridge in a lidded jar or container for up to 1 week.

VEGAN EGG

Not all egg substitutes work the same—some are great for binding, like flax and chia, and some for fluff, like aquafaba. Here are three options that replace eggs in vegan cooking and baking that you'll see throughout this book.

Flax Egg

For each egg, put 3 tablespoons of hot water in a small bowl and whisk in 1 tablespoon ground flaxseed. Allow the mixture to thicken, 5 to 8 minutes. You may store prepared flax eggs in a lidded container in the fridge for up to 1 day.

Chia Egg

For each egg, put 3 tablespoons of hot water in a small bowl and whisk in 1 tablespoon whole chia seeds or 2 teaspoons ground chia seeds. Allow the mixture to thicken, 5 to 8 minutes. You may store prepared chia eggs in a lidded container in the fridge for up to 3 days.

Aquafaba

For each egg, use 3 tablespoons of aquafaba (see page 27 for more on aquafaba).

Substitutes

Instant PLANT MILK

This is all you need to know about homemade plant milk: 1:3. It's the golden ratio of oats and/or nuts to water to create the creamiest, smoothest bev every time. I like to get creative with my oat/nut combinations to make milk flavors that I can't buy elsewhere. You can definitely skip the vanilla, sweetener, and/or cinnamon. Lots of and/ors here, so just remember: 1:3.

Makes
3¼ TO 3½ CUPS (26 TO 28 OUNCES) PLANT MILK

3 cups cold water

⅔ cup old-fashioned rolled oats

⅓ cup nuts or seeds, such as almonds, cashews, pistachios, sunflower seeds, pumpkin seeds

Pinch of fine sea salt

1 teaspoon maple syrup (optional)

¼ teaspoon pure vanilla extract (optional)

Pinch of ground cinnamon (optional)

1 In a blender, combine the water, oats, nuts, and salt. Blend on high for 1 minute or until the oats and nuts are completely pulverized. Add in the maple syrup, vanilla, and cinnamon, if using, and blend again.

2 The strength of your blender and the blending time will affect the smoothness of your milk. Also, if you want your milk to be even smoother, more like a commercial plant milk, you can strain it through cheesecloth or a fine-mesh strainer.

3 Once the milk is strained, store it in a lidded bottle or beverage container in the fridge for up to 1 week.

TWO-INGREDIENT (NO BANANAS!) ICE CREAM (PAGE 170) made with VEGAN CONDENSED MILK (PAGE 202)

Condensed milk is like a thick, sweet syrup that is used in a lot of chewy desserts. Although you can find veganized coconut condensed milk varieties at some specialty stores, they can be hard to come by. This homemade version is simple enough and can be used to make my Two-Ingredient (No Bananas!) Ice Cream (page 170) or as a sweetener for coffee, tea, oatmeal, and anything you can think of.

**Makes
1¾ CUPS**

½ cup organic cane sugar

¾ cup plus 2 tablespoons water

2 teaspoons vegan butter

2 cups raw cashews, soaked in water to cover overnight and drained

1 In a small saucepan over medium heat, combine the sugar and the 2 tablespoons water. Heat, stirring, until the sugar has fully dissolved, 2 to 3 minutes. (You don't want to overcook it, as it will become solid again!) Remove the sugar syrup from the heat and stir in the butter until it's melted. Set aside to cool.

2 In a blender, pulse the cashews several times. Then add the ¾ cup water in three parts, blending after each addition. Pour in the cooled syrup and blend for another 30 seconds, until the mixture is very smooth and creamy, almost like a thick milkshake.

3 Chill in the fridge for at least 1 hour before using, and store in a lidded jar or container in the fridge for up to 1 week.

VEGAN *Condensed* MILK

APC (ALL-PURPOSE CHEESE)

Smooth, stretchy, chewy, delicious. A good vegan cheese is hard to come by, and as much as I'd like to veer away from the cashew-based varieties because of how often these nuts are used in dairy-free replacements, they make for the perfect mozzarella substitute, and no other nut works quite like them. Check out my bright green Personal Pizza (page 136) for some margherita inspiration, or use however you would enjoy your favorite cheese.

Makes
A SCANT 1-CUP (JUST UNDER 8 OUNCES) BALL OF CHEESE

1 cup raw cashews

1¼ cups cold water

3 tablespoons tapioca starch

2 tablespoons freshly squeezed lemon juice

2 tablespoons nutritional yeast

1 teaspoon sriracha

¼ teaspoon fine sea salt

Few pinches of freshly ground black pepper

 1 In a small saucepan over medium-high heat, combine the cashews with 1 cup of the cold water and bring to a boil. Lower the heat and gently simmer for 10 minutes.

 2 Strain the boiled cashews. Then add them to a blender with the remaining ¼ cup water, tapioca starch, lemon juice, nutritional yeast, sriracha, salt, and pepper. Blend on high, stopping to scrape down the sides of the blender as necessary, until a smooth, spreadable paste forms, like a slightly thinned nut butter.

 3 If you have a nonstick skillet, use that to cook the cheese. If you don't have one, it's okay, but get ready to soak the pan before you clean it because the cheese will stick some.

 4 Using a rubber spatula, scrape the smooth nut mixture into a nonstick skillet or saucepan and cook over medium heat, folding the mixture constantly with the spatula, until the paste becomes a smooth ball and it turns a darker shade of gold, like the color of smoked mozzarella, about 5 minutes.

 5 Let cool. Then slice or shred to use. Refrigerate whole, shredded, or sliced for up to 4 days in a resealable container.

Potato CHEESE

It seems most vegan cheeses are made using nuts, right? Not this one! Behold, the simplest, tastiest homemade cheese recipe. Inspired by pommes aligot, a French dish combining cheese and potatoes to create a stretchy, sophisticated mashed potato, this cheese is made using a similar technique, with a few extra ingredients to help it set in the fridge. You can melt it on nachos (it grates well straight out of the freezer), use it in wraps, or eat it right from the fridge. (When it's cold, it reminds me of Babybel—you know, those little pillowy round cheeses wrapped in red wax.) Warm or cold, this cheese smacks. For a colorful twist, use purple potatoes instead of white.

Makes
ABOUT 2 CUPS

2 baking potatoes (about 1½ pounds), steamed (see Get Steamy with Taters!, below)

2 to 4 tablespoons pickle juice or freshly squeezed lemon juice

2 tablespoons Instant Plant Milk (page 199) or unsweetened oat milk

2 tablespoons tapioca starch

2 tablespoons neutral oil, such as safflower

1 teaspoon garlic powder

1 teaspoon onion powder

½ teaspoon paprika

½ teaspoon turmeric (omit for white cheddar)

½ teaspoon fine sea salt

¼ teaspoon freshly ground black pepper

1 First, scrape the insides of the steamed potatoes into a blender. (Reserve the skins for snacking later, or see Garlic and Onion Potato Peel Crunches, page 43.) Next add the pickle juice, plant milk, tapioca starch, oil, garlic and onion powders, paprika, turmeric, salt, and pepper to the blender and pulse until smooth.

2 Transfer the mixture to a nonstick skillet and cook over medium heat, stirring constantly, using a heatproof spatula, until it starts to bubble and thicken, 5 to 8 minutes.

3 Remove the cheese from the heat and let it cool. Transfer the cooled cheese to a container with a lid. Store in the fridge for up to 1 week or in the freezer for up to 3 months. Slice, melt, shred, and enjoy.

⭐ Get Steamy with Taters!

To steam potatoes, pierce them several times with a fork and put them on a microwave-safe plate. Place the potatoes in the microwave and cook on high for about 7 minutes, or until you can pierce them easily with a fork (not like the pierce felt *before* you cooked them!).

Makes
1 CUP

7 ounces (about ½ block) firm or extra firm tofu, drained and at room temperature

3 tablespoons Homemade Vegan Mayo (page 196) or store-bought vegan mayo

2 tablespoons nutritional yeast

1 tablespoon freshly squeezed lemon juice or vinegar

1 tablespoon seltzer water

*A **classic, creamy spread.*** This cream cheese substitute has a smooth texture you might expect from a non-vegan version, and it takes no time to make. I like eating it with Bubble Bagel Bites (page 83) or Two-Ingredient Pretzel Cloud Bites (page 48), and it can be subbed in any recipe that calls for cream cheese, like my Granola Cheesecake Bars (page 180). Add herbs, veggies, caramelized onions, or anything you can think of to make custom flavors.

 In a blender, combine the tofu, mayo, nutritional yeast, lemon juice, and seltzer water. Blend on high until very smooth, scraping down the sides as needed.

 Transfer the mxiture to a lidded container, smoothing the top with a spatula, and refrigerate for at least 2 hours before using. Store in the fridge for up to 2 weeks.

TOFU
Cream
Cheese

BUTTERY *Spread*

Vegan butter can be expensive, which is why I created this homemade alternative. It melts just like the real thing and is dairy- and oil-free. I spread it on toast and use it for baking. Although it doesn't panfry and crisp up foods as butter does, it's a great thickener and creamy addition to stir-fries, sauces, and soups.

Makes
ABOUT ½ CUP

1 (13.7-ounce) can coconut cream, chilled in the fridge overnight

1 to 2 tablespoons fresh squeezed lemon juice

1 tablespoon nutritional yeast

¼ teaspoon fine sea salt

1 teaspoon dried oregano (optional)

1 Scoop the coconut solids from the top of the can (use the remaining coconut liquid in oats or smoothies, or discard) into a blender or food processor. You should get about 1 cup. Add 1 tablespoon lemon juice, the nutritional yeast, salt, and oregano (if using). Pulse until smooth and fully combined, with a texture like a thick hummus. If you'd like your spread to be a little tarter, add the second tablespoon of lemon juice.

2 Spoon the mixture into a piece of cheesecloth and wrap well or tie to secure. Place in a strainer over the sink and weigh down with a bowl or pot. Let the liquid drain from the mixture for 1 hour; then give the cheesecloth one final squeeze.

3 Transfer the spread to a lidded container and put it in the fridge to solidify. Keeps for up to 1 week.

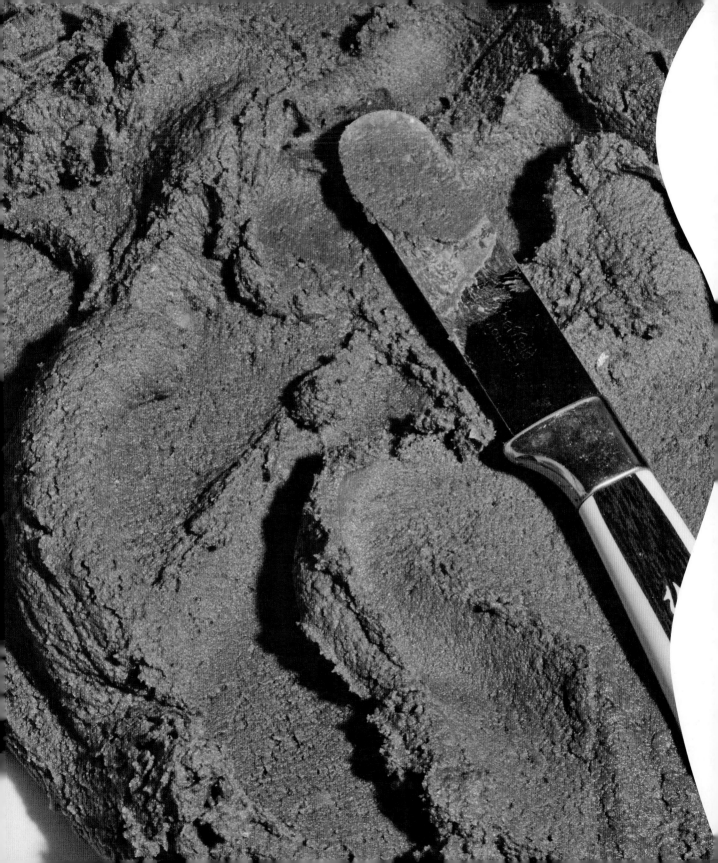

1 (15-ounce) can chickpeas, drained and rinsed

⅓ cup Cheap & Sweet Syrup (page 194) or maple syrup

⅓ cup dark unsweetened cocoa powder

1 to 2 tablespoons refined coconut oil, melted

½ teaspoon pure vanilla extract

¼ teaspoon fine sea salt

1 to 2 tablespoons nut or seed butter (optional)

This spread has the whipped, creamy texture of hummus combined with the sweet and chocolaty flavors of a dark chocolate bar. I love it on fresh fruit, as a sandwich filling, or even as a pre-workout or midday snack right off the spoon. Using canned chickpeas makes this an easy one—it takes about five minutes to prepare and can be enjoyed instantly. The best part? You don't even taste the beans.

 1 Place the drained chickpeas between two towels or paper towels and lightly apply pressure to roll them around, removing as many skins as possible.

 2 In a blender, combine the skinned chickpeas, Cheap & Sweet Syrup, cocoa powder, coconut oil, vanilla, salt, and nut butter (if using). Pulse the blender on high, scraping down the sides between pulses, until the mixture becomes a smooth paste. Add more salt or oil to taste.

 3 Store in a jar or airtight container in the fridge for up to 4 days.

Chocolate PROTEIN Spread

TRAIL MIX *Butter*

Recently as I was walking through the spreads section of the grocery store, I realized just how many things—nuts, seeds, oats, cookies—are now spreadable, so why not trail mix? The addition of dried fruit adds a tartness to this nutrient-packed spread. Plus, you can customize this recipe to include your favorite trail mix additions and make it your own.

Makes
ABOUT ¾ CUP

½ cup old-fashioned or quick oats

½ cup raw mixed nuts

¼ cup neutral oil, such as grapeseed or safflower, plus more as needed

2 to 3 tablespoons maple syrup

1 tablespoon chia seeds

1 tablespoon flaxseed

1 tablespoon dried fruit of choice

1 tablespoon vegan chocolate chips

Pinch of fine sea salt

1 Preheat the oven to 325°F.

 Spread the oats and nuts evenly on a sheet pan. Bake until the nuts become fragrant and start to turn golden, about 18 minutes. (You won't see a change in the oats, and that's okay.) Let cool.

 In a blender, combine the toasted oats and nuts, oil, maple syrup, chia seeds, flaxseed, dried fruit, chocolate chips, and salt. Blend on high until smooth, stopping often and scraping down the sides of the blender as needed. You may have to do this six or seven times to reach your desired consistency. Add more oil if needed for a thinner spread.

 Store in a lidded jar or container at room temperature for up to 2 weeks.

DIY Snack To-Go
MASON JAR VEGGIES

This is what I like to call stupid simple. Mason Jar Veggies
are a mix of your favorite vegetables and dip, cleverly
placed in a portable jar to be eaten in the car or straight out
of the fridge when you're in need of a quick snack, or to be
stashed in your bag for later.

CHOOSE YOUR SPREAD OF CHOICE:

**2 to 3 tablespoons
Trail Mix Butter
(page 210)**

**Ranchy Dressing
(page 192)**

**Your favorite nut
butter**

**Kale Pesto Crumble
(page 224)**

Your favorite hummus

USE ANY OF THE FOLLOWING:

Bell peppers

Carrots

Celery

Snap peas

Pretzel sticks

Veggie straws

Apples

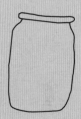

Spoon your spread of choice into the bottom of an 8-ounce lidded
mason jar and spread it with a rubber spatula.

Rinse, peel if necessary, and cut any of the fruits or vegetables
you are using to fit in the jar.

Secure closed with the lid and store in the fridge or take on the go.
I usually make 5 to 7 jars to last the week.

NUT-FREE

Makes
ABOUT ⅔ CUP

½ recipe (1 cup) Spiced Oat Flour (page 215)

¼ cup refined coconut oil

¼ cup Cheap & Sweet Syrup (page 194) or maple syrup

½ teaspoon pure vanilla extract

Fine sea salt

A huge shout-out to Oat Haus's Granola Butter, which they developed as the world's first oat-based spread. It's not quite nut butter, not quite cookie butter. Instead, it's the ideal graham-y happy medium. This is my own version, and it is addictive.

1 In a blender, combine the Spiced Oat Flour, coconut oil, Cheap & Sweet Syrup, and vanilla. Blend on high until smooth and creamy. Taste and season as needed with salt. Blend again.

2 Store in an airtight container at room temperature for up to 2 weeks.

GRANOLA Butter

DIY *Oat Flour*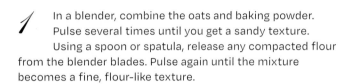

This flour is very simple to make and is one of my favorite substitutes for all-purpose flour when I'm cooking or baking gluten-free. I love using it in cookie dough recipes so I can eat the dough raw, but that's just me (maybe you, too?).

Makes
2 CUPS

2 cups old-fashioned rolled oats

1 tablespoon baking powder

 In a blender, combine the oats and baking powder. Pulse several times until you get a sandy texture. Using a spoon or spatula, release any compacted flour from the blender blades. Pulse again until the mixture becomes a fine, flour-like texture.

2 Store in an airtight container at room temperature for up to 3 months.

SPICED *Oat Flour*

Use this warming combination of cinnamon and nutmeg in your flour as a flavorful sub for plain oat flour in both sweet and savory recipes, such as my Nut-Free Granola Butter (page 212) or French Toast Fries (page 78).

Makes
ABOUT 2 CUPS

2 cups old-fashioned rolled oats

2 tablespoons flaxseed

1 tablespoon ground cinnamon

1 teaspoon ground nutmeg

 In a blender, combine the oats, flaxseed, cinnamon, and nutmeg. Pulse several times until you get a sandy texture. Using a spoon or spatula, release any compacted flour from the blender blades. Pulse again until the mixture becomes a fine, flour-like texture.

2 Store in an airtight container at room temperature for up to 3 months.

Sweet Potato Dough

1 medium sweet potato (about 1 pound), steamed (see Get Steamy with Taters!, page 204), peeled, and mashed until smooth (save the skins for Garlic and Onion Potato Peel Crunches, page 43)

1 cup all-purpose flour

¼ teaspoon fine sea salt

Tofu Dough

7 ounces (about ½ block) firm tofu, drained

1 cup all-purpose flour

½ teaspoon fine sea salt

Procedure for both doughs: In a medium bowl, stir together the sweet potato or tofu, ¾ cup of the flour, and the salt until a crumbly mixture forms. Using your hands, bring the dough together, squeezing it in your palms, to form a ball.

Once a ball is formed, sprinkle 2 tablespoons of flour on the counter or workspace and knead the dough until it becomes smooth and bounces back when you gently press your finger into it, working in the extra flour on the counter.

Keep working the dough until it becomes sticky, another 2 to 3 minutes, then sprinkle the remaining 2 tablespoons flour on the counter and continue to knead until the dough becomes smooth and bouncy once again. When you press it lightly with your finger, the depression should bounce back.

Use immediately or wrap in plastic wrap and refrigerate until ready to use. The dough will keep in the fridge for up to 2 days.

SWEET POTATO   TOFU   GF AVOCADOUGH

These two-ingredient doughs are staples. No water needed. Simplicity at its best. The sweet potato dough is one of my all-time favorites and inspired the other two. You can use these to make Snipped Tofu Pasta (page 127), Sweet Potato Tortillas (page 218), Avocadough Crackers (page 46), and so much more. Feel free to get creative!

GF Avocadough

You can always use regular all-purpose flour here, too.

1 ripe avocado, halved and pitted

¾ cup gluten-free all-purpose flour

½ teaspoon fine sea salt

2 tablespoons water, plus more if needed

Scoop the avocado pulp into a medium bowl and mash it well with a fork. Stir in the flour and salt until a shaggy dough forms. Try bringing the dough together with your hands. If it is too crumbly to stick together, add a tablespoon of water and knead once again until it sticks together. You may need to add an additional tablespoon of water. Knead the dough until it is smooth and pliable.

Use immediately or wrap in plastic wrap and refrigerate for up to 1 hour. (Because of the nature of avocado, this dough does not hold past an hour.)

Use Your Dough!

TOFU DOUGH:
- Tofu Pops (page 22)
- Tofu-Shell Taco Night (page 111)
- Snipped Tofu Pasta (page 127)

TOFU DOUGH OR SWEET POTATO DOUGH:
- Easy Homemade Pastas (page 126)

TOFU DOUGH, SWEET POTATO DOUGH, OR GF AVOCADO DOUGH:
- Sweet Potato Tortillas (page 218)

GF AVOCADOUGH
- Avocadough Crackers (page 46)

Sweet Potato

Nothing beats a homemade tortilla. You can also make these using Tofu Dough (page 216), as I do for Tofu-Shell Taco Night (page 111), or GF Avocadough (page 217).

Makes
6 TORTILLA SHELLS

½ batch Sweet Potato Dough
(page 216)

Flour, for rolling out

2 teaspoons extra-virgin olive
oil, plus more as needed

1 Divide the Sweet Potato Dough into 6 equal pieces and roll into small balls. Lightly flour your work surface, and using a rolling pin or bottle, roll out each piece one at a time into a 5-inch round tortilla. Lay them out on a sheet pan. (Don't stack them, as they may stick to one another.)

2 In a medium skillet over medium-high heat, add 1 teaspoon of the olive oil. Then cook the tortillas one by one until little bubbles appear on the surface, about 1 minute 30 seconds. Flip and cook until golden spots appear on the underside, another 1 minute 30 seconds, adding more oil if needed as you cook. Transfer the cooked tortillas to a plate lined with a damp cloth, wrap, and set aside until ready to eat.

3 Store in a plastic bag for up to 1 day. Reheat in a warm skillet for a minute or two before serving.

TORTILLAS

Emergency BREAD

"I'M OUT OF BREAD!!!" That used to be me when I didn't have bread. If you're ever in the same predicament, or just in the mood for a single-serving English-muffin-like instant bread recipe, try this out. Obviously, there's nothing like a well-risen, proofed, and freshly baked loaf, but this tasty option with a somewhat spongy texture will certainly do in a pinch, and it's a great way to satisfy a craving for carbs!

Makes
1 ROLL/VERY MINI LOAF

¼ cup all-purpose flour

1 tablespoon ground flaxseed

¼ teaspoon baking soda

1 to 2 generous pinches of fine sea salt

2 tablespoons Instant Plant Milk (page 199) or plant-based milk of choice

1 teaspoon extra-virgin olive oil

¼ teaspoon white vinegar

1   In a small bowl, stir together the flour, flaxseed, baking soda, and salt until combined. Add the plant milk, olive oil, and vinegar and stir until a shaggy dough forms. Using your hands, bring the dough together to form a small dinner-roll-like ball.

2   Place the ball in a small microwave-safe cereal bowl or dish, and zap on high until the dough bounces back when lightly pressed, or 1 minute. It's best to test the bread at 1 minute, then cook longer at 10-second intervals if needed. The dough turns rock hard if overcooked.

3   Eat as a roll/English muffin, or slice, toast, and enjoy. If you are eating this later, pop it in an oven preheated to 425°F to crisp up the crust, 2 to 5 minutes.

☆ Emergency Bread Dip

In a small bowl, whisk together 2 tablespoons olive oil, 2 tablespoons balsamic vinegar, and a pinch each of fine sea salt, black pepper, and red pepper flakes. Dip and enjoy!

GO-TO *Baked* GRANOLA

Because of its versatility, granola is hands down one of the best breakfasts and snacks to have on hand. You can use it as cereal, as topping on a smoothie bowl, as a hearty crust, or just to enjoy by the handful. This version is not only chunky, crunchy, and easy to make, but it keeps throughout the week. When I buy granola, I don't want a bag of crumbs. Homemade is the answer. No time to bake? Check out my Chunky Cocoa-Banana Stovetop Granola (page 69).

Makes
ABOUT 2 CUPS

2 tablespoons almond butter or nut butter of choice

2 tablespoons Cheap & Sweet Syrup (page 194) or maple syrup

2 tablespoons Instant Plant Milk (page 199) or plant-based milk of choice

1 prepared vegan Chia or Flax Egg (page 198)

1½ teaspoons pure vanilla extract

2 cups old-fashioned rolled oats

1½ teaspoons ground cinnamon

1   Preheat the oven to 350°F. Line a sheet pan with parchment paper. Set aside.

2   In a large bowl, whisk together the almond butter, Cheap & Sweet syrup, plant milk, Chia Egg, and vanilla until smooth. Add the oats and cinnamon and toss to coat.

3   Pour the oat mixture onto the prepared sheet pan and spread out in a thin layer with no spaces between the oats. Using the back of a spatula, press it down firmly (this is what will help give you chunky clumps). Bake until the oats start to turn golden around the edges, about 20 minutes. The oats will continue to dry and get crunchy as they cool.

4   Remove from the oven and allow to completely cool before breaking into chunks. Store in an airtight container for up to 1 week.

☆ Spice Notes

Feel free to play around with spices in this cinnamon-forward granola. Do you like your mix a little less cinnamony? Reduce it to ½ teaspoon. Or omit and add ⅛ teaspoon of ground nutmeg, or use both. Or how about cardamom or turmeric? Or even chili powder or smoked paprika. Get spicy!

One thing about me: I don't buy jam. I like to make my own, because then it's not too sweet, and I add chia for extra nutrition. I can also adjust the texture by altering the cooking time—for a spread or filling (this works great in my Small Pie, page 182), I add an extra 5 to 10 minutes. For a thinner fruit puree topping, I cook it less than the suggested cooking time. Make it yourself and fix it just how you want!

Makes
1 CUP

2 cups frozen mixed berries

3 tablespoons chia seeds

1 to 2 tablespoons Cheap & Sweet Syrup (page 194) or maple syrup

2 tablespoons fresh-squeezed lemon juice

1 In a medium saucepan over medium heat, cook the frozen fruit until softened, 10 to 12 minutes. Using the back of a potato masher or wooden spoon, mash the fruit and stir in the chia seeds, Cheap & Sweet Syrup, and lemon juice. Continue to cook the fruit mixture, stirring often, until the liquid evaporates, the mixture thickens and bubbles, and most of the fruit is broken down, 5 to 7 more minutes.

2 Transfer to a lidded jar or airtight container and let cool and thicken at room temperature for 1 hour before using or store in the fridge for up to 4 weeks.

MIXED BERRY Chia JAM

KALE PESTO

This pesto is magical. I add more oil for a classic jar pesto feel, and less for more of a kale crumble, which is great tossed on pasta or in a salad because of its chunky texture. Since I've been making pesto at home, I use it for so much more than saucing. I use it to step up toasts, as a dip for veggies, and an addition to hummus to name a few.

Makes
1¼ TO 1¾ CUPS

2 cups packed kale leaves

1 cup roasted and salted pumpkin seeds

¼ cup packed fresh basil leaves

1 garlic clove, coarsely chopped

1 tablespoon fresh-squeezed lemon juice or white vinegar

¼ teaspoon red pepper flakes

¼ teaspoon onion powder

¼ teaspoon fine sea salt

½ to 1 cup extra-virgin olive oil

1 In a blender or food processor, combine the kale, pumpkin seeds, basil, garlic, lemon juice, pepper flakes, onion powder, and salt. Pulse until a crumbly mixture forms.

2 Stream ½ cup of the oil into the blender or food processor with the blade running for kale crumble. For a saucier pesto, continue to stream in the remaining ½ cup oil (1 cup total).

3 Store in a jar or airtight container in the fridge for up to 3 days.

Crumble

CHICKPEA *Crunches* ™WO WAYS

When I'm craving something crunchy, I reach for these crispy beans to toss on salads, to top tacos, or even just to eat alone. You can easily make these crunches sweet, too, by tossing the chickpeas with cinnamon or cocoa and sugar. Feel free to get creative; the cooking time will remain the same (and don't skimp on the baking time, or the chickpeas will not get crispy!).

Makes
1½ CUPS CRUNCHES

For Savory Chickpea Crunches

1 (15-ounce) can chickpeas

1 tablespoon extra-virgin olive oil

1 tablespoon smoked paprika or curry powder

1 teaspoon fine sea salt

For Sweet Chickpea Crunches

1 (15-ounce) can chickpeas

1 tablespoon extra-virgin olive oil

1 tablespoon organic cane sugar

1 teaspoon ground cinnamon or cocoa powder

Pinch of fine sea salt

1 Preheat the oven to 400°F.

2 Drain the chickpeas and rinse (see Save the Bean Juice!, page 27, for what to do with the liquid). Place the chickpeas between two towels or paper towels to dry, rubbing off any loose skins. (Although it's tedious, try to get off as many skins as possible for crispier chickpeas.) Discard the skins. Transfer the chickpeas to a medium bowl.

3 **If making Savory Chickpea Crunches:** Drizzle the chickpeas with the olive oil and sprinkle with the smoked paprika and salt. Using a spoon, toss to coat evenly and pour the chickpeas onto a sheet pan, spreading them in a single layer.

4 **If making Sweet Chickpea Crunches:** Drizzle the chickpeas with the olive oil and sprinkle with the sugar, cinnamon, and salt. Using a spoon, toss to coat evenly. Pour the chickpeas onto a sheet pan and spread them in a single layer.

5 For both types of chickpeas, bake until the shells crack and turn golden brown, 28 to 35 minutes, shaking the pan halfway through the cooking time to unstick them. Some beans may start to pop in the pan, too!

6 Allow the chickpeas to cool before eating, as they crisp up more as they cool. The crispy chickpeas can be stored in an airtight container for up to 2 days.

This is a great way to eat quinoa if you are not a fan of the steamed version. Quinoa prepared this way is light and crispy and adds a satisfying texture to foods that need a little oomph. I especially like sprinkling quinoa crunch on salads, but recently I've been using it as a breakfast topping or mixing it with chocolate to make my own cereal or crunch bars. I find it best to use white quinoa, because you'll find it easier to see when the quinoa is done baking—the dark golden color is much more noticeable than if you use darker quinoas.

Makes
ABOUT 1 CUP

2 cups cooked quinoa

3 tablespoons extra-virgin olive oil

½ teaspoon fine sea salt

½ teaspoon freshly ground black pepper

1 Preheat the oven to 400°F.

2 Put the quinoa on a sheet pan and drizzle with the olive oil. Toss to coat. Sprinkle with the salt and pepper and toss again. Spread the quinoa out in an even layer and bake, tossing every ten minutes, until it turns dark golden and crispy, about 25 minutes.

3 Allow to cool before using. Store in an airtight container for up to 1 week.

 ### Quinoa Crunch for Sweet Treats!

When using Quinoa Crunch for something sweet, like Quinoa Crunch Cereal (page 101), I replace the olive oil with avocado or coconut oil, and leave out the salt and pepper.

SAVORY QUINOA Crunch

VEGAN Magic WHIP

FINALLY, *a vegan whip that* isn't made from coconut cream or aquafaba! This recipe is dairy-free, thick, and creamy, and holds its shape better than any other version I've tried. It uses the same emulsification method as my Homemade Vegan Mayo (page 196), but the addition of sugar and vanilla gives it a flavor like vanilla icing that is oh so good! Be sure to use refined coconut oil, too, if you want a neutral flavor. (You'll get a distinct coconut flavor with unrefined oil.) Can I describe the consistency as sexy? I'm going to, because that's how it feels to me—smooth and rich as any and all whipped creams should be.

 Makes
ABOUT ¾ CUP

½ cup unsweetened soy milk or oat milk, warmed in the microwave or stovetop

⅓ cup refined coconut oil, melted

¼ cup organic confectioners' sugar

½ teaspoon pure vanilla extract

1 In a blender, combine the soy milk and the oil. Run on high until the two liquids are emulsified—that is to say, when you dip a metal spoon into the mixture, it coats the spoon, and when you look at a spoonful, no oil is visibly separated from the milk. Refrigerate the mixture overnight.

2 Transfer the chilled milk-oil mixture to a large bowl, and using a stand or hand mixer, whip on high speed until the mixture becomes fluffy, adding the sugar a spoonful at a time as it thickens. Finally, stir in the vanilla.

3 Use immediately or refrigerate for use that same day.

Recipes to Look Out For

If you're interested in gluten-free recipes, ones which can be made without an oven, or some that can be cooked in an air fryer, here are some handy lists to get you started.

Gluten-Free

Recipes that are naturally GF, or can easily be made GF

- Puffed Beans (*page 20*)
- Sexy Tuna Salad (Fish-Free) (*page 27*)
- Rice Paper Bacon Snack Strips (when made with gluten-free soy sauce) (*page 28*)
- Kale Puffs (*page 31*)
- Chips, Chips, and More Chips (*page 32*)
- Cucumber Bites (when served with gluten-free soy sauce) (*page 37*)
- Angry Edamame (when Angry Sauce is made with gluten-free soy sauce) (*page 38*)
- Garlic and Onion Potato Peel Crunches (*page 43*)
- Moon Cheeze (*page 45*)
- Avocadough Crackers (*page 46*)
- Baby Carrot Fries (when Hal's Everything Seasoning is made with gluten-free panko) (*page 50*)
- Hand-Pressed Protein Bars (*page 54*)
- Cinnamon Granola Bark (when made with gluten-free oats) (*page 56*)
- Fluffy Vegan Omelet (*page 60*)
- Cinnamon Sugar Tortilla Bowl (when made with a gluten-free tortilla) (*page 64*)
- Chocolate Shell Smoothie Bowl (*page 66*)
- Chocolate Shell Fro-Yo Cup (*page 68*)
- Chunky Cocoa-Banana Stovetop Granola (when made with gluten-free oats) (*page 69*)
- French Vanilla Oatgurt (when made with gluten-free oats) (*page 70*)
- A Toast to Toast (when made with gluten-free bread) (*page 72*)
- Brown Sugar 'Nana Toast (when made with gluten-free toast) (*page 75*)
- Banana Peel Bacon (when made with gluten-free soy sauce) (*page 76*)

No Oven Needed

Recipes that don't involve an oven or a stovetop

Try the Air Fryer

Recipes that work great (or even better) in the air fryer

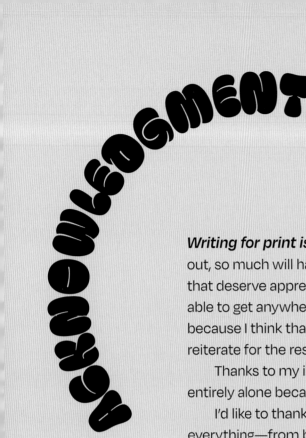

ACKNOWLEDGMENTS

Writing for print is scary, because I know by the time this comes out, so much will have changed, and there will be so many instances that deserve appreciation on a page in a book. I wouldn't have been able to get anywhere in life without my mom and dad, so I'll start there, because I think that's a well-earned thank-you that I will continue to reiterate for the rest of my life.

Thanks to my internet community, wherever you are. I've never felt entirely alone because of you, and I'll never feel alone because of you.

I'd like to thank my cowriter, Rebecca Ffrench, for literally everything—from brainstorming to testing to offering me life advice at this weird point in my life. Thank you to Brittany Maxwell, Katherine Latshaw, Justin Schwartz, Lauren Volo, Mira Evnine, Maeve Sheridan, and Megan Litt for the opportunity to create this tangible creative world of food, stories, and recipes.

I'd like to give a special shout-out to Amber Ellington, Danielle Adelstein, and Sofie Heger for testing and reviewing so many recipes in the early stages of recipe testing.

Finally, thanks to my best friends Mary Grace, Emily, Delaney, Morgan, Rose, Virginia, Jake, and Kyle, and to my siblings Heather, Harry, and Hunter for existing and advising and making fun and reminding me that despite the unique and creative and incredible space that social media is, real life will always be just a little bit better.

Index

NOTE: Page references in *italics* indicate photographs.